A LITTLE BIT

OF

GODDESS

A LITTLE BIT
OF
GODDESS

AN INTRODUCTION TO THE
DIVINE FEMININE

AMY LEIGH MERCREE

STERLING ETHOS
New York

STERLING ETHOS
New York

An Imprint of Sterling Publishing
1166 Avenue of the Americas
New York, NY 10036

Text © 2019 Amy Leigh Mercree
Cover © 2019 Sterling Publishing Co., Inc.

ISBN 978-1-4549-3670-1

Distributed in Canada by Sterling Publishing Co., Inc.
c/o Canadian Manda Group, 664 Annette Street
Toronto, Ontario M6S 2C8, Canada
Distributed in the United Kingdom by GMC Distribution Services
Castle Place, 166 High Street, Lewes, East Sussex BN7 1XU, England
Distributed in Australia by NewSouth Books
University of New South Wales, Sydney, NSW 2052, Australia

For information about custom editions, special sales, and premium and corporate purchases, please
contact Sterling Special Sales at 800-805-5489 or specialsales@sterlingpublishing.com.

Manufactured in Canada

2 4 6 8 10 9 7 5 3 1

sterlingpublishing.com

Cover design by Elizabeth Mihaltse Lindy
Interior design by Gina Bonanno

Image Credits
Illustrations by Shutterstock.com: Bourbon-88 (spiral goddess); satit_srihin (border)

CONTENTS

DEDICATION

This book is dedicated to my ancestors, those who came before and paved the way, and to the continuum of goddesses who have been with me through thick and thin. Thank you.

INTRODUCTION

Welcome to the Temple of the Divine Feminine. It is *everywhere*. It's within you. It's all around you. It's in the eyes of your daughters, in the hearts of your sisters, in the hugs of your female friends. It's in the womb of your mother. It's in the body of planet earth—the mother of our human race.

The Divine Feminine is symbolized by the Great Goddess. She knows all and sees all; she is the feminine incarnation of divinity. The Divine Feminine is sacred, and you are sacred because you embody her. She is the Great Mystery. She is the sun, the moon, the earth, the stars, the sky. She is interconnected through all that exists. She is the atoms and molecules that make up the matter of our world. She is the energy and the light flowing through every dimension. She is everything.

You might read this and think that I am talking about the Christian concept of God, but I'm not. Nowadays, the patriarchy gets a lot of airtime. This book does not intend disrespect or disregard for any religious or philosophical beliefs. This book is about tolerance. It is about honoring all aspects of the divine and advocating for inclusivity.

That being said, because those in power have promoted religious factions that focus on masculine divinity for some time, we see a tremendous amount of gender inequality in our world. Even now, we watch things unfold in our country and all around the globe that are potentially disrespectful of the feminine. Some of us may choose to stand up against this disrespect and fight for those less fortunate.

These women who take a stand are incarnations of the goddess, just as every other woman is. The ACLU lawyer suing over gender inequality aligns with the archetype of the independent and powerful goddess Athena. The social worker who counsels children who have been marginalized and brings them nurturance and justice aligns with many aspects of the mother goddess Isis.

Every day, all around the world, women honor the Divine Feminine in their own ways—often among friends and quietly. These behind-the-scenes goddesses can be the beautiful Latina mothers who sing songs about the Mother of the Moon to their pregnant friends or the radiant African women who perform rituals for health among the girls and women in their families. The stately British woman who teaches her niece about the mythology of Avalon honors the goddess, as does the American who mentors the younger women in her office and teaches an informal class on femininity in relationships every Wednesday over wine and dessert. The Divine Feminine is present in women all over the world.

The Divine Feminine brings love, nurturance, compassion, sensuality, beauty, wisdom, confidence, and so much more. As the Divine Feminine reemerges in the Western world, perhaps we will see peace in our time. We will watch the strides that women make as they let the power of the Great Goddess flow through them.

The Dalai Lama once said that the world would be saved by the Western woman. That's you. By reading this book, you will reconnect on an even deeper level with your Divine Feminine nature. Through small conscious acts of honoring the goddess within, you help tip the balance of power from a patriarchal, male-dominated place to one of equality where the Divine Feminine and the Divine Masculine are on an equal footing, together creating a world of peace.

You are part of this change. When you align with the over-arching goddess and all the goddesses we'll talk about in this book, you will find your life enhanced in myriad ways. You will find support and sustenance and spiritual food from the Sacred Feminine.

When I was twenty-three years old, I got a tattoo of the *ankh*, the Egyptian symbol of life, tattooed in an orangey brown color (the color of Indian henna) on my left big toe. I had just started working as a medical intuitive. I knew that the left side of the body symbolizes the Divine Feminine and the big toe and the thumb symbolize the idea and energy of the will. My tattoo symbolized my decision to merge my will with the will of the goddess and to do that for the highest good of all life. This included my own highest good, but it was also a decision and a statement to be of service to the Divine Feminine.

Since that day, my life has been blessed. I've had fortunate experiences such as swimming with wild humpback whales and through pristine underwater caves, hiking in verdant rain forests, climbing pristine peaks, holding and witnessing the birth of the babies of sweet friends, dancing with joy among sister goddesses, experiencing great passion and immense love with captivating lovers, meditating deeply with the great spirit, and much more.

I've learned lessons that taught me essential things on my spiritual path and in my life. I've had surgeries, experienced heartbreak, seen great friends and family pass on, and faced adversity just as we all do in different ways. Every blessing and challenge is part of the experience of learning about the Great Goddess in all her forms. She is all things: lover and mother, creator and destroyer, innocent and wise woman. She is an adventuress and a safe space, a source of knowledge and a driver to seek experiences. She is a heart opener and mind expander.

All those life events have aligned me to live my dharma, which is my life's mission—and if we talk about it in trendy terms, we could even call it the idea of "living my best life." I want this concept for you, too. I want you to have the most soul-affirming, ecstatically joyful life. I wish for you peak experiences and transcendent moments.

You are the architect of your life, and you can call in reinforcements any time you want. You can choose to align with your life's purpose and ask for the blessing of the Great Goddess. Her wisdom and energy can propel you to new heights of experience and joy.

You deserve this peak level of living. You're a masterpiece created by a universe of benevolence. The divine feminine within you is part of your true self. Every part of you, the heights and depths of you, is loved by the sacred feminine. You are all things. You matter. The fact that you are here on Earth matters. Let the essence of your inner feminine flow through you to the world. We all have a little bit of goddess within us.

❖ 1 ❖

HISTORY OF THE DIVINE FEMININE

OVER TIME, GODDESSES HAVE BEEN FORGOTTEN to some degree. They have been looked upon as secondary. Often, goddesses have taken a backseat to the more conventional—meaning societally approved—male deities. A lot has been written about the past and present of gods and a singular god, but it may be time to put some well-deserved attention on the massive historical and cultural impact goddesses have had. Because long before there was a singular god there were many goddesses, and in fact, for much of early history, humanity lived as more of a matriarchy than a patriarchy. Women gave life, and that ability was revered and heralded for the magnificent feat it was.

The origin of the goddess mythology dates back to the earliest traces of humankind, beyond the influence of a purely patriarchal-based belief system. Men, in fact, had very limited representation as deities, mainly being seen as the sons or lovers of goddesses. The earliest calculations of goddess worship date between 20,000 and 30,000 BCE in a period known as the Paleolithic. This ancient worship was observed through reverence of the color red for its connection to menstruation and rebirth, and that color often was used in ceremonies. These early societies also modeled the interior of their temples and sacred caves after female sexual organs by using shells.

The subsequent Neolithic period produced some of the most intricate goddess-worshipping sites, which can be found in Anatolia, Turkey, and date back to 6500 BCE. This period is also interesting in that it observed the similarity of life-giving properties that both women and the Earth shared. It is no coincidence that the Earth is often referred to as "mother," because it really does provide all that is necessary for existence and growth. The Earth and women were known as life givers. Possibly as a result, the images of goddesses began to appear with parts of nature, such as plants, animals, and streams. Women during that time were tasked as gatherers in their hunter-gatherer tribes and further informed this idea of a benevolent provider, as the killing of animals was left to the men. This shows the functionality and structure of matriarchal societies: Women contributed greatly to the makeup of civilization and culture, developing the arts, medicine, and rules, but they did not necessarily dominate men.

Goddesses often were attributed to specific phenomena, ideas, or virtues. Some are identified with a single, very specific concept, whereas others are considered to be a Great Goddess type, overseeing many different aspects of life. Different themes associated with goddesses include childbirth, motherhood, love, beauty, war, the moon, creation, and death, among other things. In the early view of women, often they were seen to govern individual maturity and spiritual life as well as the heart. In this, we see the flow of the life cycle at the will and creation of the female figure, and so it becomes a common theme throughout history.

In the absence of a written language, the existence of goddesses is preserved in cave drawings that depict the birth-giving ability of these deities and in carved miniatures that portray their figures, such as the Neolithic Venuses, including the Venus of Willendorf. These figurines emphasize the features of a nursing mother to show fertility and the nourishment her body provides. The word *goddess* itself starts to appear in the English language as early as the mid-1300s and soon after is adapted into many other languages.

What was once limited to a strictly Mother Earth goddess in primal times later became an all-encompassing, all-powerful heavenly mother, as in the case of Nut, the Egyptian goddess of the sky, as civilizations were established. This continued to sustain the idea of physical and spiritual connection to a divine entity's womb, as it became apparent that a divine mother created all above and below us and that people were connected to the Earth and space. Once this distinction was made and embraced in various societies—the Celts, Romans, Greeks, and Egyptians—goddesses and gods took on a much more prominent role in those cultures.

Temples have been around since the dawn of time—interestingly, those temples often were reserved to honor male deities in the Neolithic period, and the worship of female deities actually took place in the homes of those early people. This shows a much more personal and warm connection associated with these goddesses and their placement in everyday lives, as opposed to the separate and confined areas where one was expected to worship gods. Eventually, goddess temples were established for worship and prayer.

The hierarchy of the Temple of Delphi was unlike that in modern places of worship. For one thing, the most spiritually elevated person there was a woman. A female high priestess known as the Pythia or the Pythoness, named after the dragon the Greek god Apollo slew to appease her spirit, acts as a mediator between the gods and mortals, often guided by an altered state of being.

That prophetic trance is popularly believed to have been achieved through vapors emitted into the room that high priestesses, sitting on the tripod at the center, would breathe in and be raised to a different level of consciousness. However, research has shown that the presence of a vent at Delphi for exactly this purpose has not been found, even with testimony from a Delphic priest by the name of Plutarch who described the fumes: "as if the adyton [sanctuary] were sending forth the essences of the sweetest and most expensive perfumes from a spring," reporting that there was indeed a distinct scent in the air at Delphi. If the presence of fumes cannot be explained, this presents the possibility that different methods were employed, notably the use of oral hallucinogens such as plants to alter the oracle's state of mind.

The oracle had the task of being the translator between the divine and humankind, often providing answers for personal issues in common citizens' lives. This title would be passed down from one woman to another at the end of her life, and so there would always be a living resident providing this service at the temple. In addition to her duty to Delphi, the Pythia enjoyed the immense beauty of nature as it touched Greek culture in the unique atmosphere of the temple. This is yet another instance of the human meeting the "otherness" on an equal plane of existence and of the woman bridging the connection between the earthly and the divine.

Matriarchal societies provided so many benefits outside the spiritual realm. The most outstanding fact is their limited, if nonexistent, history with long-term warfare. They were considered highly peaceful cultures, built on open fields and focused on the cultivation of the arts, which were seen as divine.

Why did the world start to move toward a monotheistic, patriarchal belief system and throw out the old ways? Much of that came from the squandering of old-world practices and beliefs to promote traction and spread the belief in new gods, or rather "God." Because of the nature of female-oriented societies, which was largely seen as peaceful, their survival in an aggressive and armed new world was nearly impossible.

Despite their dismissal in the face of colonization and the modern day, the cultural relevance of and reverence for goddesses throughout time remains. Often paired with a male counterpart to show equal importance in the manifestation of the world, goddesses became integral to understanding the nature of the physical and spiritual world.

SEASONAL CELEBRATIONS OF THE GODDESS

THE WAY WE SEE LIFE, IN ALL ITS STAGES, CAN BE witnessed in the course of a single year. Within a year, we see a story of birth, evolution, gradual decline, death, and rebirth. It is a story that has followed humankind since creation. When we look at the seasons in a traditional sense, the year is divided into four parts: spring, summer, autumn, and winter.

Those names are more common in the modern age, but historically the different seasons have been distinguished by the natural phenomena observed, such as shift in the hours of daylight or the fertility of the land, known to be marked by a solstice or equinox. An association with the divine has arisen in the passage of the year when we examine the full scope of the changes the seasons bring. Many seasonal celebrations were formed from a long and venerated set of customs and traditions that in some cases are very specific to certain regions of the world and in other cases prove to be surprisingly universal across different continents.

SPRING

Spring is known to be a time of growth and renewal. This is especially apparent in the rich abundance of the planet as flora and fauna replace the lifeless aftermath of winter's frost and in the awakening of animals from their months of quiet rest who come out to seek the warmth of the sun.

Spring has always been seen as a period of prosperity for life and as an indicator of balance. The vernal (spring) equinox takes place on March 20 in the northern hemisphere and September 20 in the southern hemisphere. It is one of two days in which there are equal hours of day and night. This phenomenon has been observed across various religions and cultures.

The theme of rebirth, which spring is characterized by, is seen in the Christian tradition of Easter. In the Bible it is known as Jesus's resurrection from the dead, taking place three days after his burial and being held on a Sunday.

Beyond this view of the holiday by Christian standards, Easter can be seen as a modern celebration of pagan holidays. In fact, the word Easter is believed to be rooted in the name of the Teutonic goddess Eostre, who is the goddess of fertility and spring. There were so many names for the Great Goddess in her springtime/dawn form: Eostre, Ostara, Inanna, Persephone, Eastre, Ishtar, Freya, Bridgit, and hundreds more. Those goddesses and many more were celebrated at this time of year in festivals to honor the dawning light. They were typically fertility goddesses, and rabbits and eggs were powerful symbols to denote flowering, plenty, and sensual love. They were part of the modern idea of spring fever. Modern-day Easter is a wonderful day to embrace newness and enjoy the sweetness of the season of blossoms as bestowed by the life-giving divine feminine.

The tradition of Beltane, or May Day, comes from the Celtic calendar and is historically celebrated on the first day of May, right between the spring equinox and the summer solstice. It symbolizes the coming of summer, and it was a day on which the pastoral Celtic people attempted to shed the darkness of the previous months by lighting great fires to cleanse themselves and the wildlife. As it was celebrated throughout Scotland and Ireland, people would drive their cattle over the flames and some people would even dance on it. May bushes, which were normally hawthorn or sycamore trees, would be danced around and decorated. Beltane was at times also a glorious celebration of sensual love. In some traditions, ritual mating would occur and was reported to be sensuous, sacred, and renewing. In some cultures, a priestess of the goddess would couple with a reigning monarch to bless the kingdom or town with the fruitfulness of the ripe goddess. This was observed at times in the temples of beautiful goddesses of sensual love, including Isis, Inanna, Ishtar, and various Celtic deities. Sexuality was not shameful in those times but a celebration of the idea of the sacred marriage of the Divine Masculine and the Divine Feminine. This could be enacted as love-making or meditated upon as an act of internal alchemy, merging the inner masculine and feminine for a fruitful life full of blessings.

In later Celtic iterations of May Day, young women symbolizing the Maiden archetype of the Great Goddess would wear fresh flower crowns made in a ritualistic manner and dance joyfully around a maypole. Often, the village people would join in this jubilant floral festival and dance. The idea was to celebrate the renewal of spring and honor the Great Goddess and her bestowals to come in blooming and harvest times.

SUMMER

The summer solstice is recognized to occur on June 21 in the northern hemisphere. It is a day that has more hours of daylight than of darkness. The power of that fact found its way into the celebrations of different civilizations. The sun for many societies and cultures embodied life-giving properties and life itself as the summer proved to provide fertile land for crops and thus provided more vegetation for livestock that would be consumed by people.

In ancient Rome, the summer solstice was the occasion for another unique exception to everyday life: On the first day of the festival of Vesta or Vestalia, married women could, for one day only, enter the temples of the Vestal Virgins. There they would be allowed to make offerings to Vesta, the goddess of hearth and home. Summer goddesses of bloom such as the Roman Flora and Fortuna also were celebrated at this time.

FALL

Autumn is another transitional point of the year and is marked by the autumn equinox on September 23. In the autumn equinox, the northern hemisphere once again receives an equal number of daylight and nighttime hours.

Samhain comes halfway between the autumn equinox and the winter solstice to mark the end of the Gaelic harvest season. It originated in Celtic and Gaelic traditions. The coming of the darker half of the year is anticipated and acknowledged with this marker. It typically starts on October 31 and ends the following day, November 1, at sunset. Can you think of a modern holiday that shares this date? You guessed it—Halloween! Halloween actually has its origin in the Samhain tradition. You can see how certain holidays are changed and adapted to fit the coming of new ages and people.

Interestingly, although this holiday is about the darker half of the year, it is not a scary or ominous experience but rather one in which the binaries of life and death are observed in the space of darkness. Samhain embodies the cycle that life goes through, the order and chaos of the universe.

Honor the Divine Feminine within you on Samhain. For many millennia, during this time of year after a plentiful harvest as the air cooled and days got shorter, it was believed that this evening brought our closest connection with the spirit world.

The symbols of harvest that were used to celebrate included pumpkins, gourds, squashes, and apples. It was believed that ancestors brought blessings for the next year. On altars to honor those ancestors, sweets, the equivalent of candy at that time, were placed to treat those beyond the veil. On this Samhain evening, we honor the goddess in her wise woman form. The goddess is within you as well as woven through the world surrounding you. On Samhain night, full of moonlight and potential, see her beauty all around. You are the goddess.

Samhain is the night to honor those who came before us. The veil between the worlds is thin, and we have the opportunity to connect with our benevolent ancestral guides. Just make sure that you always ask for everything to be for the very highest good of all life and in accordance with universal natural law—helping all and harming none. Allow yourself to feel the blessings of Samhain.

WINTER

Norse, Germanic, and Celtic Yule or Yuletide began on the winter solstice, which we know as December 21, the shortest day of the year. This day was thought to herald the return of the sun and, symbolically, the light within. During the sun's yearly journey, its return begins on the solstice as the days lengthen. The Greeks held a festival to commemorate Dionysus at this time, and the Romans celebrated the god Saturn then as well. Yuletide was typically a three-day and three-night celebration. It started on December 21 and usually culminated with a feast on December 24. This was known as the Yuletide Festival. It was a celebration of the birth of the actual, physical sun from the Great Goddess. It was believed that the goddess gives birth to the sun.

For the Yuletide Festival, many symbols from the natural world were used. The evergreen tree was symbolic of youth and returning life, and it was also the symbol of everlasting life. The evergreen was brought into the home in some areas of the United Kingdom and Europe, eventually becoming the Christmas tree we know so well. The evergreen denoted rebirth and the birth referenced as the sun was being born again. The goddess gives birth to the sun in everlasting life because each year the sun is reborn.

Holly was a symbol of the time of year up to the solstice. Its symbolism is similar to that of the evergreen tree because it is an evergreen family plant. It has a life-giving aspect, but it also has spikes for protection. Newborn babies were sprinkled with water that had been infused with holly. Some people think that the idea of holy water was passed down from the earlier practice of using holly water. Holly plants would be soaked under a full moon overnight, and then the water would be sprinkled over babies for protection. This practice was especially popular in Germanic cultures. It was sacred to the German version of the Greek goddess Persephone; her plant was the holly berry.

After the winter solstice, the oak tree was a prominent symbol as the sunlight returned. Mistletoe was thought of as a healing and protective plant. In some traditions, it is never supposed to touch the earth, and so it was hung instead. It was meant to be between sky and earth. The berries on mistletoe were white and were supposed to represent fertility; thus, people would kiss under it. In mystery schools and goddess temples, specifically those in the United Kingdom but also those throughout Western and Eastern Europe, it has been reported that mistletoe was ingested. It was hallucinogenic, and so people would use it to induce visions and shamanic journeys.

Ivy is another symbol of everlasting life and resurrection. It was thought to exist between the worlds of heaven and earth. Pine (evergreen family) trees were thought to bring healing and joy into the home, and so some who celebrated Yule burned boughs to infuse the home with purity. Wreaths were made out of the evergreen plants to symbolize the wheel of life. They were hung on doors and laid on altars with candles. This was the origin of the Christmas wreath.

The Yule tree, a pine typically, was decorated for the Festival of Saturn in Rome. Romans and Celtic people would bring a live tree into the home so that the wood spirits would have a place to keep warm in the winter. They would leave food and drink on the branches for the spirits; that was how they'd decorate the tree. Lighting of candles was popular at Yule because it was about departing from the darkness and entering the light as the sun was reborn. Red and green were popular colors because of the red holly berries and the evergreens, and gold was symbolic of the sun. As you can see, many Christmas traditions come from this. In Germanic, Anglo-Saxon, and Druidic traditions, people gave celebratory gifts because it was the birthday of the sun.

The end of the three-day Yule celebration was usually a feast. In Rome, it was the feast of Mithra (born of the goddess Anahita). In Greece, the god Apollo and his twin sister, Artemis, were born of their goddess mother, Leto. Apollo was another deity associated with the sun and rebirth who was celebrated in a multiday festival beginning at the winter solstice. In Norse mythology, Odin was celebrated at the same time. He was married to the powerful goddess Freya, also known as Frigga and Frigg. Odin was born of the goddess Bestla. Odin was also a symbol of the resurrected sun/son born of the Great Goddess.

The study of mythology need no longer be looked on as an escape from reality into the fantasies of primitive peoples, but as a search for the deeper understanding of the human mind. In reaching out to explore the distant hills where the gods dwell . . . we are perhaps discovering the way home.

—H. R. ELLIS DAVIDSON,
GODS AND MYTHS OF NORTHERN EUROPE

✦ 3 ✦

MAIDEN, MOTHER, WISE WOMAN

THE ROLE OF THE GODDESS AND OUR RELATIONship with the divine feminine has changed so much that it is a sometimes forgotten part of human history. Many traditions and concepts that developed in the time of goddess worship have been erased or painted over. The pagan idea of the Triple Goddess, however, continues to survive and sustain itself. What exactly is the Triple Goddess model? You might be surprised to know that you can very well recognize it in modern times—it has been taken and adapted into concepts within religions, one example being the Holy Trinity in Christianity.

It is believed that European pantheons mirrored the characteristics attributed to the Triple Goddess in the stages of the moon, which resulted in the worship of many moon goddesses throughout ancient civilizations. The Triple Goddess also is reflected in the life cycle of a woman: our childhood as a girl, our growth into adulthood as a young woman, and finally a stage of restfulness and meditation as an older woman. In the original model of this cycle of a woman's life, maidenhood replaces childhood, young adulthood means embracing the role of a mother and lover, and the wise woman, also known as the crone, has all of life's experiences and wisdom. This isn't an exclusive rite of passage just for women; the concept of the Triple Goddess is meant to show the natural stages of life: youth, maturity, and old age. The Triple Goddess was honored by men, women, children, and the elderly as an ideal course of life.

The figure of the Triple Goddess is, for all intents and purposes, a singular deity. You can think of each part of the Triple Goddess, however, as a face, and with each face comes a set personality, traits, and characteristics. The unity of this idea can teach us all we need to know about enriching our lives through love, respect, peace, and harmony as we view the planes of existence that each one of us eventually will face. The importance of honoring the Triple Goddess lies in the fact that she brings an understanding that no matter what stage in life we are in, we must embrace others to live a happy and full existence. Much of this understanding is something innate, within us. The Triple Goddess is the face of human life and is something we are familiar with in our everyday lives, even something that we may carry unconsciously. By looking toward the Triple Goddess directly, you can mobilize great change from within that will then translate to a lasting and positive impact on the world around you.

MAIDEN

The Maiden represents all the youth and potential for growth that is shown in the earliest stages of life. She is the beginning of life, often associated with spring for her birth and rebirth at the start of every new cycle. Referring back to the time when the aspects of the Triple Goddess were connected to stages of the moon, the Maiden is tied to the waxing moon stage, which is significant because it is the beginning of menstruation and puberty.

It is in this stage that the world is unfamiliar and beautiful. The Maiden aspect is curious, an adventurer in the new world; as a result, she also is called the Huntress. As is often the case with youth, the Maiden is open and untamed in her emotions and actions, as they fall within the rules dictated by the Mother.

Another name by which the Maiden might be referred to is the Virgin. In this case, Virgin does not correlate to sexual virginity. Virgin in this sense is an identity as a free and independent being, with no one to comply with but herself. This doesn't mean that she lacks concern for others. She is actually a champion for all creatures and promotes conscious empathy for all beings.

It is in the Maiden that we connect with our independent spirit and zeal for newness. We can use this archetype frequently to help us embody curiosity, enthusiasm, and the strength of youth. Following is a selection of some of the many goddesses that we identify with the Maiden archetype. Keep in mind that some goddesses embody more than one archetype, such as being a Maiden and a Mother.

Artemis

The Greek goddess of the moon, Artemis is one of the best and most popular examples of the Maiden archetype. She is also widely known as the goddess of the hunt in Greek culture and is said to have taken an oath of eternal maidenhood. She is a protectress of the wilderness, children, and young women. She is a very strong and adventurous goddess.

Brigit

The goddess Brigit was known throughout Western European countries as an independent goddess who specialized in healing, fire, and prophecy. An all-female priesthood of nineteen priestesses maintained a fire year-round at her sanctuary in Kildare. Brigit, also known as Brigid and Bridget, can share her courageous spirit and fiery self-assurance with us when we connect with her.

Athena

Athena is widely known as the Greek goddess of wisdom, and her other domains are the arts and justice. She also has been recognized as a goddess of women's rights and freedom. In her characterization as a Maiden, she opposes the needlessness of violence, despite the way statues of that time portrayed her in battle gear.

Ixchup

Ixchup, also known as Young Moon Goddess, is a little-known Mayan goddess. She is married to the Mayan sun god but maintains a status of maidenhood for her ties to the young phase of the moon. She can connect us with new ideas and possibilities.

Danu

The Celtic goddess of fertility, Earth, and wisdom, Danu is a figure with great intelligence and a vastly loving heart. She helps us cultivate metal and emotional strength. She is also a deeply spiritual goddess and the mother of the Irish mythological race the Tuatha Dé Danann, who are thought to have transformed themselves into leprechauns after the Roman invasion of their land in historical times.

Libertas

Libertas is someone you might be familiar with if you have ever seen a picture of or visited the Statue of Liberty. Libertas is the Roman goddess of freedom and greatly embodies the idea of the Maiden with her call for independence. She helps us find our liberty and inner freedom, and she accepts all peoples without judgment and with open arms.

Eostre

Eostre is the Maiden of spring, celebrated in Anglo-Saxon cultures. She was known in Germanic cultures as Ostara. The modern-day holiday Easter began as a festival honoring her newness in springtime. She symbolizes the rites of spring and the freshness of flower buds and blossoms. She helps with fertility, reproductive health, and the enjoyment of romantic love.

MOTHER/LOVER

The Mother aspect is the next face of the Great Goddess. It demonstrates development from the previous state and also an ability to create. Traditionally, the Mother figure was simply a mother and wife, but she also can be seen through a more modern lens as a lover and creator. She is associated with the summer season, when plants are at their ripest and life is at its fullest. The Mother aspect of the goddess is the climax of cycle, for this is the point at which she has the greatest potential for creating. This lends itself to the idea of conceiving and carrying children in this stage for women, but this is also the stage of highest production of artistic and innovative endeavors for all people.

The Mother aspect is defined by her acceptance of moving into adulthood. Childhood changes into adulthood when responsibilities are realized and acted on. Her commitments are both to others and to herself, and both are important to uphold. Creation doesn't happen without a measure of careful attention, steadfast discipline, and unbounded love—the Mother aspect of the goddess teaches us to uphold those traits and use them in all situations. We can turn to her when we are stuck and need to finish something.

The Mother aspect is representative of a relationship with love. It is in the Mother that the ritual essence of every form of love, including spirituality and acts of kindness, is found. The mother is also the Lover. This aspect is also one that contains many of the goddesses of love and sensuality. The Lover is unbounded in her passion, her seductiveness, and her desirability. In her highest form, she seeks unbridled creative union. She can create ecstasy of all kinds, whether sexual, romantic, creative, or even career-oriented. She is passion and pleasure and power. She is a love goddess. She knows how to please herself and those she chooses to favor with her skills as a partner. She is empowered and confident in who she is and in her ability to create love, lust, and whatever she desires.

The creative aspects of the Mother/Lover are intrinsic to our success. Women are kicking butt and taking names in the workplace nowadays. We're inventing things, curing diseases, and leading with aplomb. In part, that is because we're harnessing our creative abilities more than ever before. We're empowering ourselves through these archetypes.

Hsi Wang Mu

Also known as the Queen Mother Wang in Chinese culture, Hsi Wang Mu is the goddess of eternal life. Mother to all, she is also the matron goddess of women. She is honored when a girl is born.

Flora

Flora is the Roman goddess of flowers and nature. Her connection to fertility and her ability to grow organic matter tie into the creation aspect of a Mother deity. Flora also can embody the archetype of the Lover with her ability to share her abundant beauty as she chooses.

Haumea

Haumea, also known as Mother Hawaii, is celebrated in Hawaiian culture as the goddess of fertility and childbirth. She actually gave birth to another Hawaiian goddess, Pele, a Lover goddess of fire and volcano. Mother Hawaii is therefore the matron of the islands for all that she has created there.

Chalchiuhtlicue

Mainly known as a goddess of water sources, including lakes, rivers, and streams, Chalchiuhtlicue is an Aztec goddess who also is portrayed as being connected to childbirth. This comes from the concept of the amniotic sac breaking and the water of life bringing forth a new soul.

Nut

Highly venerated in Egyptian culture, Nut is called the mother of all the gods. She is the personified night sky created through her love with the Earth god. Not only is she a nurturing goddess, she is also a sensual goddess. Her union with the earth and the passion and beauty she shared overarch the world.

Oshun

Oshun is an African/Yoruba goddess of romantic love and the sea. She embodies the Lover archetype. She is sensuous and beautiful. She is desired by many and sovereign of herself. She is powerful and makes decisions and creates at will. She is adept in the art of love-making. She can help infuse our lives with sensual enjoyment and passionate ecstasy. In some traditions, she is attended by a group of three handsome young men who help her share and embody the art of pleasure and feminine enjoyment.

Queen of Cuba

The Queen of Cuba is a maternal figure. She is thought to protect women, and if you are given a gift with her image or find it unprompted, she will bring you good luck and watch over you. She is an iteration of the Mother archetype and is associated with a copper mine where she was said to have shared a miracle.

WISE WOMAN

The last face of the goddess is that of the Wise Woman, who encompasses a full life and all the earned wisdom of that life. This aspect of the Triple Goddess is sometimes the scariest to people—it symbolizes the end of a cycle. The Wise Woman symbolizes the coming of new life because cycles do not truly end but only start over. Death is a transformative event.

The Wise Woman carries with her memories, both good and bad, and the wisdom that they can provide. She represents a stage at which people can mindfully slow down and appreciate all that has occurred in their lives. It is in this way that people in their older ages can be of service to their community.

A healthy way to look at the role that the Wise Woman plays in the Triple Goddess is as a great recycler of information, energy, and organic matter (when we inevitably come to the final end), all which find their way back out into the universe to fertilize it and give it potential once again.

Hecate

Hecate is the Greek goddess of the moon and the underworld. She is a shamanic and prophetic figure and a keeper of great mysteries. She is a creator and a destroyer but also has a nurturing side. Hecate is an example of a goddess who is both Mother and Wise Woman.

Hine-nui-te-po

Known as the goddess of death in New Zealand, specifically in Maori culture, Hine-nui-te-po is also a giantess. She helps that which is ready to change form through destruction, leading ultimately to new life.

Durga

Durga is a popular goddess in the Hindu culture. She is a warrior goddess who specializes in combat. Durga is fierce and powerful. She is a symbol of the wisdom of destruction. She is a force of transformation and is benevolent to those who connect with her.

Ereshkigal

Ereshkigal is the Mesopotamian queen of the underworld, the opposite of her sister Inanna, who is queen of the heavens. Ereshkigal is a destroyer figure, a dark Mother and Wise Woman goddess symbolizing the transformative truth that all things end and are then resurrected.

Spider Woman

Spider Woman is an honored Southwestern American goddess, native to the Hopi peoples, who is a bringer of good fortune. She is revered for her wisdom and shares stories with her people.

Baba Yaga

Baba Yaga is the Slavic goddess of death. She often is portrayed as being hideous and frightening, which is a common stereotype of the Wise Woman figure as she relates to the issue of death. Death is a natural and powerful part of life.

Morgan le Fay

A principal figure in the Arthurian legends, Morgan le Fay is a great and powerful sorceress. She sometimes is portrayed as youthful but is still a catalyst for transformation through wisdom. She is a famous seer. The second sight she bestows helps us see clearly and share wisdom to move things forward according to their natural order.

EVOLUTION OF THE EVENING STAR

MANY ANCIENT CULTURES ORGANIZED THEIR mythology around the celestial bodies that were visible in the night sky. Long before we had far-reaching telescopes and sophisticated technology, humanity was looking up in wonder at the stars above us.

Myths and legends about goddesses and gods were woven through with accounts and observations of stars and planets in the sky even before it was known which were stars and which were planets.

Often, one of the largest celestial bodies, or "stars," in the sky was actually the planet Venus. For millennia, this planet has been associated with the Great Goddess. It has been linked with her aspects as lover and mother and with the idea of beauty and romantic love. That is evident in the fact that the planet was named after the Roman goddess of love, Venus.

But long before the Romans worshipped Venus, the planet was known as the Evening Star. It was frequently visible just after sunset during the time between light and dark as well as all through the night as the largest celestial body in the sky. It inspired poets and philosophers and sparked creativity and transcendence, and so it's woven through many different mythologies.

When Venus was visible at twilight with a thin sliver of a crescent moon, sometimes that crescent moon would cradle Venus the Evening Star. It was like the moon (also a feminine symbol) under the Great Goddess's feet. The symbol of the star pictured with the symbol of the crescent is used in many cultures. You will find it on numerous flags in Middle Eastern cultures and coins in European cultures, and it was once a symbol for the Ottoman Empire. But before all of that, the crescent moon nestled under the feet of the Great Goddess/Evening Star originated in a more matriarchal manner to honor and commemorate the Divine Feminine. Her symbolism lives on even though her meaning has been largely forgotten.

ANAHITA (400 BCE)

Anahita was the Persian goddess associated with the planet Venus. She was specifically associated with water and the waters of life as well as healing and fertility.

LAKSHMI (1000 BCE)

Lakshmi was associated with the planet Venus in Vedic astrology. She was known as a goddess of prosperity, abundance, and fortune. In her myth, she chose the Vedic god Vishnu as her husband. The two formed a perfect union. Many rituals are still performed in their honor, including at Hindu weddings. In this way, Lakshmi is a goddess of love and romantic abundance.

ASTARTE (3100 BCE)

Astarte was associated with the Evening Star. She is a Mesopotamian version of the queen of heaven, and her reach was far and wide as she was adopted by the Phoenicians (as Ashtart), some Egyptians, and the Canaanites (also as Asherah). She helps her devotees and all goddesses in training with romance, love, sexuality, pleasure, beauty, fertility, and inner peace through self-acceptance. Her sacred flower is the apple blossom. When you cut an apple in half horizontally, the inside arrangement of seeds forms a star. This plant and symbol were widely associated with Astarte, one of the original queens of heaven.

INANNA (4000 BCE: SUMERIA)

Inanna was a Mesopotamian (specifically Sumerian) goddess known as the queen of heaven. There was a large temple associated with her in Uruk, a major Sumerian city in what is now Iraq. Inanna bestowed blessings of love, romance, self-love and actualization, and pleasure, as well as justice and political power. The Roman goddess Libertas may have originated partially from myths of Inanna.

There is some commentary about the Temple of Inanna at Uruk as well as temples devoted to Ishtar that were called brothels. Were they? Absolutely not. The path of the priestess was a spiritual one. It was also one of the few paths available to women that did not involve marriage. Instead, priestesses learned to read (married women often did not), studied, and explored their spirituality.

Some priestesses did learn ritualistic rites that involved pleasure for both women and men. Occasionally, certain honored priestesses would participate in ritual mating with a king or a sacrificial young male. The priestess would embody the Great Goddess and grant favor to the representative of the Divine Masculine. This was thought to ensure a fruitful harvest and prosperity for the kingdom.

It is reported that Sumerian priests sang the following song to honor Inanna, the queen of heaven: "To her who appears in the sky, to her who appears in the sky, I want to address my greeting, to the hierodule who appears in the sky, I want to address my greeting, to the great queen of heaven, Inanna, I want to address my greeting, to her who fills the sky with her pure blaze, to the luminous one, to Inanna, as bright as the sun, to the great queen of heaven."

Inanna also is known for her sacred marriage with Dumuzi, her consort. They embody the divine ecstatic union of the feminine and the masculine. They help us seek perfect union in all our relationships and not settle for less than that which is soul-affirming and best for us.

ISHTAR (4000 BCE: BABYLON)

Ishtar was a much-loved Babylonian goddess of love, fertility, and justice. She was known as a strong goddess with a powerful presence. She held forth the tenets of divine love and sensual love as well as being seen as a figure of political strength and justice. She, too, was seen as an embodiment of the Evening Star. She was a powerful, robust version of the queen of heaven.

Ishtar also offered devotees the idea of sacred marriage of the feminine and the masculine within each person's being. Along with her consort, Tammuz, she embodied that sacred marriage of the masculine and the feminine. She shows us how that can be embodied by being a feminine, sensual goddess as well as a pillar of strength and power and a keeper of justice.

ISIS (2000 BCE: ANCIENT EGYPT AND PHOENICIA)

Isis is a popular iteration of the queen of heaven who was revered for centuries in Egyptian and Phoenician society and in smaller ways in early Greek sects. She was associated with the Evening Star and was a goddess of self-mastery, love, romance, fertility, beauty, and much more. She was an all-purpose goddess to many: the main incarnation of the Great Goddess and one they looked to for guidance regularly. There were numerous temples in her honor throughout what we now call the Middle East.

Isis's myth involved her consort, Osiris. In the myth, Isis travels to the underworld to retrieve the seven pieces of her lover after he has been torn asunder by his brother Set. She resurrected her love and by journeying to the darkness faced her own shadow side. She integrated herself more completely in her totality. This is a common part of Inanna, Ishtar, and Isis's myths: the journey to the underworld to retrieve seven pieces of their husbands' bodies.

With Inanna, she retrieves Dumuzi after her own sister, Ereshkigal, (a powerful goddess in her own right) dismembers him and scatters him. Ishtar retrieves Tammuz from the underworld as well. In these contexts, the Evening Star in all her beauty is also tremendously courageous because she faces her fear and does what needs to be done. How many women do you know who do this all the time? Mothers who rear their children like lionesses still feel uncertainty and fear. We all feel the depths of our own shadows, but as we call upon the Evening Star and the queen of heaven within each and every one of us, we can begin to face these challenges and find strength in the inner beauty of our feminine natures.

APHRODITE (300 BCE: ANCIENT GREECE)

Aphrodite was associated with the Evening Star and was said to have been born of sea foam. A goddess of beauty, romance, passion, and pleasure and the quintessential love goddess, she can teach us to embrace our sensuous natures and embody love in our bodies as well as our hearts, minds, and spirits. As a love goddess, Aphrodite governs romantic love, self-love, and unconditional love of the self and others. Many paintings depict her either in her Aphrodite (Greek) or her Venus (Roman) form. The most famous one is *The Birth of Venus* by Botticelli. In these paintings, she is triumphant in her victorious beauty. She is unabashedly herself.

Aphrodite can teach us to cultivate that level of self-acceptance and even a feeling of victory in simply being oneself. All people are beautiful, and Aphrodite can help empower us.

Temples of Aphrodite abounded, including the Temple of Aphrodite Urania, which still can be visited in the city of Athens. It has stood since the early fifth century BCE.

FREJA (500 BCE: NORSE)

Freja was a Norse goddess of beauty and strength who was associated with the Evening Star. She was a governess of love and passion and was a symbol for the Great Goddess and the queen of heaven to many Norse peoples. Freja was a much loved and popular goddess who was thought to be celestial in nature. As the queen of heaven she bestowed blessings upon women and children.

She also held an active principle within her. She embodies both a receptive feminine side and an active masculine nature. She was powerful and benevolent.

She and her husband, the god Odin, were the ultimate Norse power couple. Both were pillars of strength and an embodiment of the Divine Feminine and the Divine Masculine in beautiful, passionate, harmonious union and partnership.

VENUS (600 BCE: ROMAN)

Venus was a love goddess who is the namesake of the Evening Star. The goddess was thought to be the queen of heaven and was of course associated with the celestial body Venus. She was a goddess of passion and love. She brought romance and desire. She also was known to enhance fertility. She was also a powerful goddess associated with victory. She can help you embrace the divine feminine within, especially in the guise of the lover—she who gives and receives love. In some ways, the feminine is receptive and the masculine is active. Venus helps you connect to your passion (active side) and your desire (receptive side.) Your active and receptive sides combine to make you a pleasure goddess!

In the *Aeneid*, the hero, Aeneas, is guided by the Evening Star in a personified, celestial form. The author, Virgil, also cites the same star as the one that lifted Julius Caesar's spirit to heaven. This was Venus in action.

MARY (100 BCE: HEBREW)

Some accounts of the goddess known by many as Mother Mary begin with her life before supposedly bearing the mythological figure Jesus. She was thought by some to have begun as a priestess trained in spiritual mysteries in a temple of the goddess Isis. She was thought to have risen through the ranks to become the high priestess of the temple, which was also called the *Magdalene* in many temples in that time and area. Some believe her apprentice Mari succeeded her as high priestess or *Magdalene* of that temple.

She is called the queen of heaven by many in religious and spiritual traditions. Although associated with the Evening Star, she also is associated with the Morning Star that was also reported to be the planet Venus visible in the morning at a different time of year. This may have been a celestial body that was said to be noted by biblical figures.

Mary is goddess of unconditional love and infinite caring. Both a mother and lover, she brings power through nurturance and beauty. Her infinite nature as queen of heaven bestows us with love, kindness, support, and the power to embody the divine mother in all of her beauty.

✗ 5 ✗

SHE OF CLAY
AND STARS

S HE CHANGES EVERYTHING SHE TOUCHES. SHE
changes everything she touches," sang my medicine teacher's
teacher, Twyla. It was the second of three times that I had
ever met her. She had invited a select group of women to her prop-
erty in rural New England. We were instructed to wear white and
to arrive as the sun was setting. Women who must have been her
apprentices had been there all day preparing the area where the fire
would be lit at sundown.

The fire burned; it had begun as a geometric tall stack of
logs built up in a circular tower. As that tower burned down lower
and lower, Twyla sang, "She changes everything she touches. She
changes," and we all sang with her. We were singing of the Great
Goddess.

This was in the early 2000s, and I had been on my medicine
path for about five years. I had been working as a medical intuitive
for about two years. As the fire burned down, Twyla began to rake.

She transformed what was left into a carpet of glowing embers. And then we walked. We all walked across it. We stated our intentions for that All Saints' Day, November 1, the day after Samhain. It was the day Twyla said the veils were the thinnest. I walked across the burning embers twice that night. I felt the Great Goddess within me and around me and all the women in every ember. We all felt our own versions of SHE who changes everything she touches. Twyla held the door open for us all that night in concert with the spirits of her land and the many elders who had come before her.

The first time I met Twyla was at her house. She had invited my medicine teacher, Levity, and me for a ceremony. Like the fire walk that followed months later, it was held at night. It was just the three of us that evening. We gathered in Twyla's greenhouse. It was a magical place full of exotic plants and the light of the full moon. She had invited us over to do ceremony with the spirit of the night-blooming Cereus cactus in her greenhouse. Its bloom was very rare and infrequent, and this full moon would be the night. And indeed it was. There it sat in full bloom, and its aroma was intoxicating. That night, Twyla introduced the Great Goddess to me as SHE of clay and stars. The ceremony was beautiful and deep. As happens at times when we enter transcendent states, I do not remember it all. I have impressions of gentleness, femininity, receptivity, intoxicating scent, enchantment, beauty, and mystery. That night we felt the realm of the fae, or fairies, very close. We connected with the goddess Danu. She was representing the Divine Feminine. Danu adopted me that night.

I felt she was very connected to Twyla. In the medicine tradition passed down by my teacher, Levity, Twyla was like my grandmother. She spoke in her beautiful, ethereal voice as a representative of "she of clay and stars." With my inner vision, I saw the interdimensions where Danu existed. I understood in an experiential manner what Twyla meant. The Great Goddess was made of clay and stars. She came from the stars, yet her body was the clay of the earth. She is heaven and earth incarnate. You can feel her within you because she is part of you. The Great Goddess can change everything she touches. She is fluid because she is everything all at once.

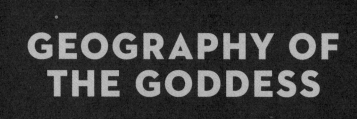

⊰ 6 ⊱

GEOGRAPHY OF
THE GODDESS

GODDESSES AND THEIR MANY VARIATIONS IN personality, attributes, and mythologies are very much tied into the cultures from which they came, and so they represent many of the ideals of these societies. There might be common themes throughout the world, such as the moon, fertility, and creation, but you'll soon realize that each goddess is uniquely her own self.

AFRICA

Africa has been shown to hold the earliest traces of humankind, and so it is no wonder that it is a repository of a vast array of unique beliefs informed and shaped by early hunting and gathering lifestyles as well as agricultural practices. Many of the myths are connected to the natural realm that people were in, with animals and spirits often being present as mythical beings with powers.

In Fon creation stories, Yewa is known as the first woman in existence on Earth, who educated her children in worship and then returned to heaven after seven years. A goddess in Fon creation known as Mawu is the goddess of the moon as well as the ruler of the night, and her twin brother rules the day. Themes of twin deities were very common in African mythology as each one represented one part of a binary to make a whole. The Yoruba people are so called because they are believed to have been the children of Yoruba, a fertility deity and goddess of the earth. The Egyptian civilization had many goddesses with whom they connected.

ASIA

The largest continent on Earth has myriad cultural traditions that formed from migrations and word-of-mouth stories and sacred texts. In ancient China, Nu Wa was known as the creator goddess as well as a fertility deity. Hsi Wang Mu, also known as Queen Mother Wang, is a goddess of eternal life, a patron of women, and the goddess to pray to for guidance and protection when a daughter is born into a family. In an interesting Indian–Chinese cultural fusion, Kuan Yin, goddess of mercy and aid in contraception, was shared by both.

In ancient Japan, goddesses had specialized roles that often embodied the lighter and happier aspects of life. Uzume is the Shinto goddess of happiness and dancing. Amaterasu is the goddess of sun and weaving, and Wakahiru-Me is the goddess of the rising sun. It is interesting to note the placement of the female figure next to the powers and energy of the sun. Benten was the goddess of music, luck, and expressiveness.

The Middle East was once full of goddess-worshipping civilizations. During ancient times the civilization of Mesopotamia thrived. It included Assyria, Babylonia, and Sumer. After that, near the same area, known at the time as the Fertile Crescent located in modern day Iraq and Iran, the Phoenician civilization also worked with goddess archetypes such as Astarte, Asherat, and Astoreth.

AUSTRALIA

Australia and Oceania, though geographically separated from the rest of the world, do not lack in diversity of goddesses and show a continuation of themes observed in other parts of the world. In Australia, origin stories and tales of journey take the limelight in the stories of Aboriginal people. The Yolngu people passed along an ancestor story of the Wagalak Sisters, who were two sisters who journeyed throughout Australia and named wildlife, plants, and places.

The islands that make up Oceania are bountiful in specialized goddesses. Hine-Te-Wauin was the Polynesian goddess of childbirth, and it was said that the spell that that goddess used to make birthing easier is still recited and practiced in New Zealand. The Maori called their Mother Earth Papa, and it was she who spread her life on Earth. Pele was the fire and volcano goddess of Hawaii and was considered one of the most powerful beings in existence in Hawaiian culture.

EUROPE

Europe is rich in a high variety of civilizations with similar themes within their ideologies, such as the Norse and Finns of the north, the Celts of the west, and the Slavs who populated the eastern part of the continent. Before the Roman Empire took hold, the Etruscans populated modern-day Tuscany, and the better-known Greeks and Romans were a major fixture in Europe. Many have different creation myths, along with the portrayal of the gods and goddesses as a family unit and the mythologies of those families and their interactions with other mythological families of the same traditions.

In the Norse tradition, Frigg is the goddess of fertility and also the queen of Asgard. She also is known as Freyja, a fertility goddess who personifies beauty and is a love goddess. According to the Finns, Luonnotar, who is known as an air girl, was the creator of the world after she dropped eggs into the water and thus formed all that is on the Earth and beyond it. The Slavs were so steeped in the family/gender role aspect of their beliefs that they even honored household goddesses such as Kikimora, who aided hardworking women, and Dugnai, who was a bread-making goddess. The Celts venerated Nantosuelta, goddess of the hearth and home. They also embodied the concept of the Triple Goddess in the Triple Mother, who is a singular being depicted as three different women.

NORTH AMERICA

Native North Americans are a diverse set of people who found their start on the continent over 12,000 years ago and gradually moved southward toward South America. Civilizations were identified by their cultural and lifestyle identifiers, and so the goddesses they worshipped reflected their realities. The Caribou Inuit people in the Arctic, for example, survived by fishing and hunting game. One of their most significant goddesses is Pinga, a hunting deity who would help direct animals to the Inuit to hunt.

Goddesses connected to food production are very common in many societies, and this makes sense with the common themes of fertility and creation that normally are associated with the female being. Native peoples who inhabited the American Great Plains venerated an agricultural goddess known as Corn Woman who made corn grow. In the same region, the goddess White Buffalo Woman was honored for her role in gathering and scattering packs of buffalo.

All throughout North and Central America, corn was seen as a staple food source. The Navajo in the Southwest recognized Yellow Corn Girl for bringing corn to them; in their culture, corn was considered a sacred plant and also was used in ceremonial events. The Aztec in Central America had numerous corn goddesses, one being Chicomecoatl, who represented stored seeds for the next year's harvest.

In Mexico and Central America, the Mayan and Aztec goddesses, such as Xochiquetzal, Ix Chel, and Coatlicue, also known as Toci, were contacted during elaborate rituals.

SOUTH AMERICA

In South America, as opposed to North America, civilizations were much more fixated on religion and the accompanying rituals. The worship of gods and goddesses was very ornate and elaborate, with large stone temples built to honor them. Mama Kilya was a beloved goddess of the moon who represented passing time and fertility. She also was called a protector of women in Inca society. It was believed that when an eclipse occurred, it was due to Mama Kilya being attacked by a great serpent. The Inca were very protective of her, and to stop this attack they would make loud noises to scare the serpent away. Chaska-Qoylor was a star deity and was honored as the sun's handmaiden. She was known as a patron of young girls.

The climate in South America, though considered tropical, actually prompted very difficult living conditions. Rain was a common theme for prayer for its importance in raising crops. Pacha Mama was an earth goddess who was second only to the sun god. She was called the giver of life and was given coca leaves as a sacrifice to help in producing good crops.

There are many beautiful, universal themes to goddess mythology throughout the world. Creation, fertility, love, justice, art, music, math, agriculture, and intuition are just some of the ways goddesses were thought to enhance life. All over the planet the divine feminine influenced life and was revered. The sacred She was part of ordinary life and a bestowal of miracles and beauty. She was nature's rainbows. She was the fruitful harvest. She was the moon and the stars above and the soil and earth below. She breathed life into babies and sustained life. She transported the dead to the afterlife. She was everything.

Now, as modern-day goddesses in training, we can learn from these traditions and create out own to share the beauty and benevolence of the divine feminine with our daughters, nieces, friends and family. Mothers who respect their feminine natures can also raise sons who treat women with care and respect and understand the interplay between the essences of masculine and feminine. When we connect with our own inner divine feminine we can live from that wellspring of inspiration. And we can pass on the ancient wisdom of the goddess.

❖ 7 ❖

GODDESS
DIRECTORY

ABUNDANTIA—Prosperity, success, abundance, good fortune; Roman/Norse

ADITI—Mother of the gods and the cosmos; Hindu/India

AERACURA—Celtic/Germanic

AMATERASU—Sun goddess and weaving; Shinto/Japan

AMMUT—Devourer of the dead; ate the hearts of the wicked; Egyptian/Egypt

APHRODITE—Goddess of love and beauty; Greek/Ancient Greece

ARTEMIS—Goddess of hunting, chastity, and maidenhood; Greek/Ancient Greece

ASHERAT—Fertility goddess; Canaanite/Mediterranean coast

ASTARTE—true sovereign of the world, mother of all star children, Pre-Christian; symbol: apple blossom

ATHENA—Goddess of wisdom, weaving, and warrior skills; Greek/Ancient Greece; animal: owl

BABA YAGA—Goddess of death; Slavic/Eastern Europe

BASTET—Goddess of sexuality and childbirth; Egyptian/Egypt; animal: cat

BENTEN (BENZAI-TEN)—Goddess of music, luck, and expressiveness; Shinto/Japan; symbol: biwa

BENZAITEN—Goddess of love; Hindu/India

BRIGHT CLOUD WOMAN—Protector of fishes; Native tradition/ American West Coast

BUFFALO WOMAN—Caused buffalo herds to scatter; Native tradition/ American Great Plains

CALYPSO—Goddess of silence; Greek/Ancient Greece

CHALCHIUHTLICUE—Goddess of rivers, lakes, and springs; also seen as a goddess of childbirth (water breaking); Aztec/Central America

CHANGING WOMAN—Creator goddess; represents the life cycle; Navaho/Southwest America

CHANG-O—Moon goddess; Ancient China; associated with moon cakes

CHASKA-QOYLOR—(Venus) a star deity, sun's handmaiden, patron of young girls; Incan/South America

CHICOMECOATL—Corn goddess, represented stored seeds for the next year's harvest; Aztec/Central America

CINTEOTL—Corn goddess; Aztec/Central America

CORN WOMAN—Made corn grow, native tradition; American Great Plains

COYOLXAUHQUI—Goddess of the moon; Aztec/Central America

CYBELE—Great Mother or mother of the gods; Roman/Roman Empire

DEMETER—Goddess of the harvest; Greek/Ancient Greece; symbol: a head of grain

DEVI—(Mahadevi) femininity; Hindu/India

DIANA—Mother of wildlife and moon goddess; Roman/Roman Empire

DUGNAI—Household goddess; helped in breadmaking; Slavic/Eastern Europe

DURGA—Warrior goddess; Hindu/India

ELEUTHERIA—Goddess of liberty; Greek/Greece

EPONA—Goddess of the earth; Celtic/Britain and Western Europe; animal: horse

ERESHKIGAL—Goddess of darkness, ruler of the underworld; Babylonian/Western Asia; creature: part vulture, part snake

ERIS—Goddess of chaos; Greek/Ancient Greece; symbol: golden apple

EVE—All living things; Christianity

FIRST MOTHER—Sacrificed herself for her people during famine; native tradition/Eastern North America

FLORA—Goddess of spring and nature; Roman/Roman Empire

FORTUNA—Goddess of chance; Roman/Roman Empire; symbols: rudder, wheel, and cornucopia

FREYJA—Fertility goddess, magic and riches; Norse/Scandinavia; symbol of sexual freedom

FRIGG—Goddess of the rain and fertility, seer of the future, queen of Asgard; Norse/Scandinavia

GANGA—Represents the Ganges, purity; Hindu/India

GEFION—Attendant to Frigg; Norse/Scandinavia

GIRL WITHOUT PARENTS—First living being, helped create the world; Apache/Southwest America

GREAT GODDESS, THE (Mother Earth)—Creator of the universe, guardian of fruitfulness, antiquity

GUINEVERE—King Arthur's queen; Celtic/Britain and Western Europe

GWENHWYFAR—First lady of Wales; Welsh/Britain

HANNAHANNA—Mother goddess, Hittite; Anatolian/Western Asia

HARMONIA—Goddess of harmony; Greek/Ancient Greece

HATHOR—Cow goddess, guardian of women and protector of lovers; Egyptian/Egypt; plant: papyrus

HAUMEA—Goddess of childbirth; Hawaiian/Hawaii

HEBE—Goddess of youth, presided over serving ambrosia and nectar; Greek/Ancient Greece

HECATE—Goddess of magic, patron of witches; Greek/Ancient Greece

HERA—Goddess of marriage and childbirth, queen of Olympus; Greek/Ancient Greece

HESTIA—Goddess of the hearth, overseer of social order; Greek/Ancient Greece

HINA—Great goddess of the Polynesians; Polynesian/Pacific Islands

HINE-NUI-TE-PO—Goddess of death, giantess; Maori/New Zealand

HINE-TEI-WAUIN—Goddess of childbirth; spell is recited to make birthing easier (still practiced in New Zealand); Polynesian/Pacific Islands

HSI WANG MU (QUEEN MOTHER WANG)—Goddess of eternal life, patron of women; Chinese/China; reason to connect: when a daughter is born

HYGEIA—Health goddess; Greek/Ancient Greece

IDUN—Spring goddess; Norse/Scandinavia; symbol: apples of youth

INANNA—Queen of heaven, goddess of rain and moonlight; Sumerian/Iraq and Sumer, Bronze Age

IRIS—Goddess of rainbows, messenger of Hera; Greek/Ancient Greece

ISHTAR—Fertility and sexual love goddess, star of the evening, identified with the planet Venus; Babylonian/Western Asia; sacred animal: lion. In the Sumerian form, she was the goddess of war and the star of the morning

ISIS—Birthed sun/moon, heaven/earth, female/male, divine wisdom, created the Nile; Egyptian/Egypt

IXCHEL—Lady Rainbow, goddess of all things and pregnancy, could foretell the future; Mayan/Central America

JANAÍNA—Also known as Yemanja, goddess of the ocean; Yoruba/Brazil

JUNO—Goddess of all, patron of marriage and women; Roman/Roman Empire

KALI—Pure female energy, protector of the universe, womb

KAMRUSEPA—Goddess of healing and magic; Hittite, Anatolian/Western Asia

KI—Earth goddess, mother of the gods and mortals; Sumerian/Western Asia

KIKIMORA—Household goddess, aided hardworking women; Slavic/Eastern Europe

KORE—Blessed Death, holds the keys to lower and heavenly worlds; pre-Greek

KUAN YIN—Goddess of mercy, healer; connect with to receive help in conception; Buddhist/India and China

KYLLIKI—Love goddess; Finnish/Northern Europe

LADY OF THE LAKE—Protector of humanity; Celtic/Britain and Western Europe

LAKSHMI—Goddess of good fortune and beauty; Hindu/India; attracted to sparkling jewels; people use lanterns

LUONNOTAR—Creator of the world; Finnish/Northern Europe

MAIA—Star goddess, also of spring and rebirth; Greek/Greece

MAMA KILYA—Goddess of moon, passing time, and fertility, also protector of women; Incan/South America; symbol: eclipses

MATI-SYRA-ZEMLYA—Earth goddess; Slavic/Eastern Europe

MAWU—Goddess of the moon; Fon/Western Africa

MA'AT—Goddess of truth, harmony, and justice; Egyptian/Egypt

MESKHENET—Goddess of childbirth; Egyptian/Egypt; symbol: birthing tile

MORGAN LE FAY—Fairy, Celtic; Britain and Western Europe

MORRIGAN—Goddess of war, sexuality; Celtic/Ireland; animal: raven

MUT—goddess of the sky, surrogate royal mother; Egyptian/Egypt; animal: cat or cow

NAMMU—Primeval sea, birthed the sky and earth; Sumerian/Western Asia

NANTOSUELTA—Goddess of hearth and home, water goddess; Celtic/Britain and Western Europe

NEITH—Mother goddess, invented childbirth; Egyptian/Nile Delta and Egypt; symbol: shield with two crossed arrows

NEPHTHYS—Funerary goddess; Egyptian/Egypt

NIKE—Goddess of victory; Greek/Greece

NINHURSAG—Earth mother; Sumerian/Western Asia

NINLIL—Fertility goddess; Mesopotamian/Western Asia

NINMAH—Goddess of birth, created humans; Mesopotamian/Western Asia

NUT—Goddess of the sky; Egyptian/Egypt

NU WA—Creator goddess, fertility; Chinese/China; animal: snake

NYAI RORO KIDUL—Mermaid goddess of the South Seas; Javanese/Java

OUR LADY OF CHARITY—Cuba

OUR LADY OF REMEDIES—Spain

OYA—Ruler of the Niger River, patron of female leadership and eloquence; Yoruba people/Nigeria; connect through long maroon bead necklace

PACHA MAMA—Earth goddess, giver of life; Incan/South America; common offerings: llamas and coca leaves

PAPA—Mother Earth; Maori/New Zealand

PELE—Fire goddess, hula; Hawaiian/Hawaii

PERSEPHONE—Goddess of spring, fertility; Greek/Ancient Greece

PINGA (PANA)—Hunting goddess; Inuit/Arctic region

QUEEN OF CUBA—Copper, Cuba

QUEEN OF HEAVEN (VIRGIN MARY)—Mystery and sacredness of birth

RENENET—Cobra goddess, leads the harvest and guardian of the pharaoh, can help with crop growth, prosperity, and food abundance; Egyptian/Egypt

SARASVATI—Goddess of all knowledge; Mother of the arts and language; invented Sanskrit; Hindu/India

SATI—Ideal of feminine love, reincarnated into Parvati; Hindu/India

SEA WOMAN (SEDNA)—Mother of sea beasts, protector of sea creatures; Inuit/Arctic region

SEKHMET—Punishment goddess; Egyptian/ Egypt; represented with a lion's head on a woman's body

SELENE–Goddess of the moon; Greek/Ancient Greece

SERKET—Scorpion goddess, has powers to repel evil and involved in funeral rites; Egyptian/Egypt

SESHAT—Queen of the library, scribe to the gods; Egyptian/Egypt

SHAPASH—Goddess of the sun, torch of the gods; Canaanite/Mediterranean coast

SIF—Wife of Thor; Norse/Scandinavia

SPIDER WOMAN—Brings good fortune; Hopi/Southwest America

STORM GODDESS—Can create floods; Mayan/Central America

TARA—Mother goddess, protector, first female Buddha; Tibetan Buddhism/Tibet

TARA (red, white, and green)—Hindu/Buddhist

TAWERET—Protector of women in childbirth; Egyptian/Egypt; ways to connect: wear a charm of Taweret or place mother's milk in vase and perform a good luck spell

TEFNUT—Goddess of moisture; Egyptian/Egypt; animal forms: serpent and lioness; represented by pair of splitting lips

THEMIS—Goddess of justice, known for wise and just advice; Greek/Ancient Greece

TIAMAT—Primeval chaos, saltwater ocean; Mesopotamia/Western Asia; represented as a female dragon

TRIPLE MOTHER—Carrying a dog, a fish, and a basket of fruit; Celtic/Britain and Western Europe

UKEMOCHI—Goddess of food; Shinto/Japan

USHAS—Dawn goddess, reborn every morning; Hindu/India

UZUME—Goddess of happiness, dancing deity; Shinto/Japan

VENUS—Goddess of love; Roman/Roman Empire

VENUS OF WILLENDORF—Self-impregnation, productivity, and beauty; Paleolithic

VESTA—Goddess of the hearth; Roman/Roman Empire

WAKAHIRU-ME—Goddess of the rising sun; Shinto/Japan

WAGALAK SISTERS—Named wildlife, plants, and places as they traveled; Yolngu people/Australia

XOCHIQUETZAL—Goddess of flowers and fruit, also goddess of music and ruler of part of the underworld; Aztec/Central America

YELLOW CORN GIRL—Along with her twin brother brought corn to the Navaho; Navaho/Southwest America; corn is a sacred plant in ceremonies

YEMANA—Goddess of the ocean; Santeria/Cuba; to connect: wear seven silver bracelets (or ones with blue and white beads)

YEWA—First woman in existence; Fon/Western Africa

YORUBA—Goddess of the earth, fertility deity; Yoruba people/Nigeria/Western Africa

ZORYA—Trinity of goddesses, represent dawn/twilight/midnight, guardians of the universe; Russian mythology/Russian

Welcome the world of benevolent, powerful, caring, wise goddesses. These goddesses beckon you with open arms and hearts. The diving feminine is all around and the goddesses above. There are also many more forgotten goddesses who want to know you and be there for you. To tap into the goddess's benevolence, you simply need to acknowledge her and accept her kindness and generosity. You can ask her now to help you receive your heart's desire for your highest good.

Benevolent spirit guides always respect your free will, so you have to ask for their help. You can do this easily and informally. Just talk to them. As archetypal beings of light, they seek to help humanity and specifically the essence of femininity, in any body, and any form. They are champions of the feminine and are also lovers of the masculine. They endeavor to help us create a better world. Make sure to receive their offerings with gratitude and unlock your inner goddess.

THE INNER TEMPLE

ALL OVER THE WORLD AND THROUGHOUT HISTORY there were temples devoted to the Great Goddess. For example, in the Sanctuary of Brigit in Kildare, nineteen priestesses who symbolize the nineteen-year cycle of the Celtic "Great Year" tended an eternally burning fire to honor Brigit, the powerful goddess of many things, including freshness and poetry.

Some of those temples were large and institutional, and some were simply the homes of women and men in which the power of the goddess was looked to for guidance and strength. Whether a temple is a great Greek architectural marvel or a simple village cottage, it can hold the vibration of the goddess. People have the power to use their intention, which is a combination of their thoughts, feelings, and actions, to bring things into being.

This means that even your home or your bedroom or your study or even just a little altar on a table can hold the vibration of the goddess if you choose. In addition to those external temples, you have within you the greatest temple of all—the inner temple.

For you, your physical body, your feelings, your thoughts, and your energy are temples as well. You've heard the saying that your body is a temple. This is true. And if you're a woman, that means that it's a goddess temple. You hold the power of the Divine Feminine in your form. Even if you were born male and you gender identify as a female, you hold the power of the goddess within you. We all hold the vibration of the Divine Masculine and the Divine Feminine within us.

If your inner temple is a female body, you have many of the Divine Feminine attributes, such as the ability to create life. You have the ability to nurture, hold, and feed the totality of a baby or an idea to which you give birth. Creating life also means overall creativity. Feminine creativity has a certain flavor, one in which the seed of an idea is released, nurtured, and then shared just as an egg is released from an ovary and travels to the womb to be fertilized and nurtured there; then, eventually, a baby is born.

The female body goes through stages that are representative of the Triple Goddess. Just as we talked about in Chapter 3, our inner temple is first a Maiden full of freshness and blossoms. Next, when we become the archetype of the Mother, it doesn't necessarily mean we have children, but we share creative ideas and nurture progress. Finally, we become Wise Women. Our experience informs our reality, and we share our gifts in new and powerful ways. Guess what? Age really doesn't matter. We can embody any and all of these archetypes at any age.

Our feminine energy inner temple experiences certain physical rites of passage associated with our femaleness. As we grow, when we reach the point of the onset of menses, we are initiated into a new circle of the Divine Feminine, that which is sometimes called the feminine blood ministries. At certain points in history, it was reported that all the women in a village would experience menstruation at the same time every month on the new moon. Less frequently, in other villages the same thing would happen on the full moon. Because of that, some people called the period of menstruation each month their "moon time." Have you ever noticed during your moon time that you feel more intuitive or sensitive? Do you feel more empathic or psychically open during that time?

In those villages, all the women would gather together in what was called the red tent. They would be attended to by the younger girls of the village, who would make them sweetbreads to consume as they sat and talked and laughed and told stories while resting on straw. Those sweetbreads were probably equivalent to the cakes and chocolate bars that we sometimes crave during our moon times. Physiologically, that occurs because at that point in our cycles we have our lowest progesterone levels, which can bring about very mild feelings of depression or the blues, and sweets and chocolate give us a burst of feel-good brain chemicals to combat our hormonal states temporarily.

Menopause was the time of life when women were thought to become the Wise Woman or Crone archetype. This was a time when the inner temple that is the body is calibrated to access deep inner wisdom. It is a time of potential regeneration. The inner temple and our bodies and beings as women can be full of freshness and newness at any age and conversely can be wise and sage even in youth. We can nurture at any age and live as who and what we choose. We have that power within us. In Chapter 9 you can connect with specific goddesses in creative ways.

You also can use the following all-purpose goddess meditation with any of the goddesses listed in the Goddess Directory to connect with and receive from any aspect of the Great Goddess that resonates with you at any time you'd like. Explore the goddesses and their manifestations within you and in your life!

ALL-PURPOSE MEDITATION TO CONNECT WITH A PARTICULAR GODDESS

Find a quiet, comfortable place where you will be undisturbed for about twenty minutes. Decide on one or more goddesses with which to connect. Sometimes it is good to start with one at a time. Keep a journal, a pen, and water nearby. Sit or lie down and allow yourself to take some deep breaths and begin to feel centered.

Take a deep and long inhalation through your nose. Feel the air first go all the way down into your abdomen and fill that area so that your abdomen moves outward. In that same inhalation, feel the middle part of your lungs, the thoracic area, fill, followed by your upper chest and the top of your lungs, so that the inhalation starts from the bottom and fills up your torso like a bag of air.

When you exhale, feel like you are squeezing the bag out from the top to the bottom. Your exhalation should be longer than your inhalation. Try to exhale the air in a slow steady stream. You can exhale through your nose if that is comfortable or through your mouth if you need to.

This is a simple form of complete abdominal breathing. Start repeating that breathing cycle. Do that for a few minutes.

Now bring your attention to the goddess you would like to connect with. Say aloud or in your mind, "Dear _____, I am so grateful that I have opportunity to connect with you today. I would love to get to know you and open my heart to your messages. I also ask you for a special blessing for me (and _____). I would love your help in any and all areas of my life. I have questions about _____ and am open to your guidance on that and all matters. I gratefully receive your healing, information, and light as needed for my highest good and the highest good of all life. I ask that everything that transpires in our communication be in accordance with universal natural law, helping all and harming none. Thank you."

Next, bring your hands out in front of you with the palms facing up. You can say out loud or in your mind that you invite the goddess of your choosing to hover her spirit hands above your physical hands. Allow yourself to feel the connection there. Does it tingle? Does it feel warm? Is it pulsing?

Sit in meditation in that posture with the goddess you've invited. Allow yourself to feel the connection between your palms and her palms. Allow your heart to connect with that goddess if you choose. You may feel a pulsing in the center of your chest. You may have a feeling of warmth or love flow through you. Allow yourself to go deeply within as you connect with this goddess. Allow your intuition to be open. You may feel insights or guidance spring forward in your mind. You may see pictures or colors in your mind's eye. You may hear music or sounds. You may smell an aroma or taste a certain flavor. You may get a sensation of flowers around you. Allow your senses to be open and even to mix together.

Let your intuition guide you through this process. Sit in communion with the goddess of your choosing for as long as you'd like. When you are done, make sure to thank her, and then you can bring your hands down. As you do so, you can say, "I disconnect from _____ as needed for my highest guide. Thank you so much, my dear goddess friend."

Open your eyes and allow yourself to come back into the room. Notice the sights, sounds, and feeling of the couch or bed beneath you. Breathe normally. Make sure you are fully present and then continue with your day. Be sure to drink plenty of water after any meditation activities.

Use this meditation to work with any goddess you choose. It will also work with other spirit guides, like angels. Make sure you journal about your experiences with your guides! Over years, you may see themes emerge. Sometimes you will discover you received guidance that makes sense later. I have looked back in old journals and seen that I wrote about something before it happened. This way you can remember!

❖ 9 ❖

GODDESS
MEDITATIONS
AND ACTIVITIES

THIS SECTION OF THE BOOK IS FILLED WITH GOD-dess-based meditations and activities for you to try out to connect with different goddesses. If you want to have a fun and goddess-oriented week, you can do one of these each day. Or just do one (or two!) whenever you are so moved. They're great to do at night before bed or in the morning to start the day. Keep a journal at hand so that after you enact the meditation or activity you can take notes on anything you noticed or any goddess guidance you received. It's always a good idea to drink plenty of water after meditations or activities like these. Water helps everything in the body function more optimally, including the nervous system, which is positively affected when you meditate or engage in transcendent activities.

LOVE AND PASSION

With the help of beloved goddesses, experience the meditation and activity contained in this section to bring new levels of love and passion into your life.

GODDESS OF LOVE MEDITATION

Today you have the opportunity to meditate on the concept of love. Love is a broad term that includes self-love, romantic love, unconditional love, spiritual love, and passionate love, among other things. As you meditate on the idea of love today, understand that it's an experience to be had by the physical, emotional, mental, and spiritual parts of yourself. Your soul is fed by love. Love is soul food. The energy of love infuses you with light and positivity in most cases. Love on its own is pure and perfect. When we add other ingredients to the mix, sometimes that's when we hear about love in the form of heartbreaking love songs and Shakespearean tragedies. In our meditation today, we will connect with all the positive aspects of love with the intention of improving our ability to love ourselves and enhance our loving relationships. We also will allow ourselves to experience and infuse the world with unconditional love.

Meet the goddess Janaína. She is a Brazilian deity of love and the ocean. She will be our guide today as we meditate on this idea of love. You can picture her wading in the ocean or floating above it. She sometimes is known as a mermaid goddess.

Find a quiet and comfortable place in which you can lie down uninterrupted for about twenty minutes. Relax into the space and relax your body. Make sure you're nice and comfortable so that you can really let go into the meditation. Breathe deeply into the center of your chest. Feel your lungs expand and fill completely.

Slow down your breathing and allow your body and mind to slow down and calm.

Bring your focus and attention to your brow center. With your focus there, you may feel pulsing or tingling. State aloud, "I ask that everything that transpires in the entirety of this meditation be for the very highest good of all life and in accordance with universal natural law, helping all and harming none. I now connect with Janaína. I open my heart to the love that she brings, and I'm grateful for her fluid blessing of liquid love. Thank you, Janaína."

Now bring your attention to the center of your chest. Feel it pulsing. You may sense warmth. Feel Janaína pouring light pink sparkling liquid love into your heart. Envision yourself floating on your back in an endless sea of light pink glistening, iridescent water. This is the ocean of love. Float there and envision Janaína above you continuing to pour love water over you. Maybe she's sprinkling it over you or misting you with it. The water is warm and inviting. Allow yourself to explore. You can turn over in this ocean and open your eyes and see what's beneath you. Everything in this ocean is made of pure love. Open your pores and absorb it. Let it fill you. Let it heal you. Let it stir you. Feel love for yourself and love for the world. Let yourself feel romantic love. You may feel stirrings of passionate love in your body and heart. Let everything unfold as the waves and ripples of love flow through you.

When you turn over in the ocean, allow yourself to sense or visualize benevolent, joyful dolphins beneath you. These dolphins are residents of the sea of love. Are they pink? Are they aqua? Allow them to swim around you and feel the resonance of the concept of the freedom of love flow through you. Love is free. It does not require physical proximity. It transcends space and time. Let these truths permeate you and reprogram every cell in your body and all of your energy bodies.

When you're ready, you can turn back over and see Janaína above you. You can speak to her telepathically with ease. Ask her for any blessing or favor you would like. Understand that our spirit guides love to intervene for us but cannot usurp our free will, and so we must ask for their help in many cases.

Thank the goddess and offer to serve her if she needs anything for the highest good. Stay in the space as long as you like. Let yourself receive guidance and healing from the goddess.

When you're ready, you can begin to bring your awareness back into the room. Feel yourself present in your body. Notice where you're lying. Wiggle your fingers and toes. Take some deep breaths. Drink some water. Sit up and briskly rub your hands over your feet, lower legs, hands, and forearms and say aloud, "I'm here now. I am present."

Once you are fully back to yourself, go about your day and make sure to drink plenty of water. Because of the oceanic nature of this meditation, if you have some untreated Celtic, Hawaiian, or Himalayan sea salt and you'd like to put a few grains under your tongue after the meditation, that would be perfect.

GODDESS OF PASSION ACTIVITY

The next activity is brought to you by the goddess Aphrodite. She is a famous Greek love goddess, bringing romance, passion, fertility, and beauty. This activity is designed to help you connect with the passionate nature within you. The passion that flows through you is the lifeblood of humanity. You may feel passion for your work or creative pursuits, and you may feel sexual and romantic passion. Passion is full of fervor. It's the lust for life within us all, whether on the surface or deeply buried. This energy and vigor can be part of what makes life worth living. Aphrodite will bring this to you today in whatever form is for your highest good. It might be desire or sexual passion. It might be poetry and song that flows from you in a passionate rush. It could come in the form of renewed passion for aspects of your life that have grown stale. Passion moves energy. It is kinetic. It is in motion and emotional. Allow yourself to feel it today.

Stand tall. Reach your arms up above you and feel the blessings of Aphrodite rain down upon you. Bring your arms down and begin to move your body in an undulating motion. Move your arms and legs as if you're dancing even though there's not any music playing. Keep moving, swaying your hips and undulating your body.

State aloud, "Dear Aphrodite, I invite you into all corners of my life for all time, as needed, for my highest good and the highest good of all life. I ask that everything we do together be in accordance with universal natural law, helping all and harming none. I invite you to infuse me and my life with the vigorous, joyful passion of existence. I invite you to flow the kinetic energy of engagement with life through me. I choose peak performance and peak experiences. I choose to experience ecstatic, joyous, passionate abandon in a way that is safe and healthy for me, for my highest good, and for the highest good of all life. I trust that you and all of my guides will provide me with the perfect balance of rest, relaxation, and joyous peak experiences. I choose to allow myself to feel safe and attract situations in which I can indulge in my passions in a way that is safe and holistically healthy for all involved. It is done."

Now lie down on the floor or a couch and close your eyes. Tune in to your body. How do you feel? Feel Aphrodite all around you, igniting your passion and enlivening your soul. Feel your body. Where is the energy moving and pulsing? Where is the passion reverberating in your body?

When that feels complete, bring your attention back into the room and go about your day. As you continue through the rest of the day and night, periodically bring your thoughts back to the passion that you began to feel moving through you. Notice if it informs your choices or decisions during your daily life. Notice opportunities to infuse your life with more passion. What could you do that would be more of a peak experience in each moment?

SUCCESS AND WEALTH

The meditation and activity in this section will connect you more deeply with your potential for success and activate your ability to receive abundant wealth.

GODDESS OF SUCCESS MEDITATION

What does success mean to you? Does it mean career achievement? A certain salary or profit? Does it mean a certain level of recognition or fame? Helping more people or animals? Success can mean different things to different people. One of the things I want for you as you do this meditation is to expand your idea of success. Think even bigger. Expand the possibilities of success in your mind and heart. Allow yourself to connect with what true unbridled success would feel like for you. And then go get it.

To connect with the true essence of success and your ability to step into it, we will meditate with the goddess Fortuna. She's the Roman deity of good fortune, good luck, abundance, money, success, and possibilities.

Spend a few minutes getting comfortable and cozy. Have your journal nearby to take notes after meditating. Sit or lie down in a relaxed position. Allow your mind to become unfocused. With less of a grip on your mental functioning for a few minutes, discover what comes up in your mind without prompting. Just watch it as if it's floating by on a cloud. No judgments or feelings of obligation to change what you're thinking and feeling are allowed—just complete, utter acceptance.

Now bring your awareness to your solar plexus. Find this in the center of your torso between your sternum and your belly button. You have an energy center, or chakra, there. It's like a galaxy inside you. Feel it revolving within you. You can place your hands over that area of your body to help you tune in to it. Connect with that part of yourself—it is the seat of your success and your will. This is the place from which you effect change in the world. This is the place that governs your action in this world.

Does the area feel jumpy, low-energy, high-energy? Does it feel healthy? Irritated? Balanced? Just notice. Now state aloud, "I invite the benevolent goddess Fortuna to infuse my being with the essence of success. I accept Fortuna's blessings and good fortune into my life with ease. I give Fortuna clearance to shape and mold my life and being into a joyous, fortunate, successful, prosperous form. I accept Fortuna's guidance with gratitude. I ask that all that transpires in this meditation be for the very highest good of all life and in accordance with universal natural law, helping all and harming none."

Meditate with Fortuna and feel her with you as you continue bringing your attention to that solar plexus chakra in your body. You want to optimize that area. You are powerful and wield your strength with benevolence and ease.

If you choose, you can tell Fortuna with your mind that you would like to dream with her tonight. In your dreams she can help calibrate optimal success. You may find yourself dreaming of her sending forth a golden strand of energy with which to magnetize your heart's desires. Allow Fortuna to teach you this over time.

Once that feels complete, bring your attention back into the room and make sure that you feel present. Thank Fortuna for her attention. As you continue with your day, you may feel Fortuna with you on the periphery. She is available to help you; all you have to do is ask for her help.

GODDESS OF WEALTH ACTIVITY

This next activity is all about increasing your wealth with the help of a benevolent goddess named Demeter. Demeter is a Greek goddess of harvest and a mother goddess. She reaps the fruitfulness of abundance, and you can do that, too. Demeter's blessing and energy will help you connect to a flowing stream of unlimited wealth. Money is energy, just like everything else. When you receive money, you're receiving energy. When you give money, you're giving energy. You can simplify your relationship with money by taking all your biases and cultural ideas about it and releasing them. Instead, allow yourself to expand your mind and adopt the idea that money is simply a tool that assists us in the exchange of energy. There is enough energy in the universe for everyone to have an unending surplus. That is the essence of abundance, and that is the energy Demeter will help you integrate into your body, being, and bank account.

Grab a journal or notebook and a pen or marker. Think about the color of the pen or marker. What color represents wealth to you? Some good choices would be green, purple, gold, red, and silver.

In your journal, write down the title "My Joyful Wealth Statements." Underneath that, we will create ten affirmative statements about your experience with wealth, prosperity, and money. I'm going to give you some examples, and I want you to individualize them. Remember to think big!

Choose ten of the following statements or create your own:

I AM A MONEY MAGNET.

MONEY FLOWS TO ME EASILY AND GENTLY, AND I AM AWASH IN IT.

**MY FINANCIAL LIFE IS FLOURISHING. MONEY
COMES INTO MY LIFE WITH EASE.**

MY FULFILLING CAREER EARNS ME A GIGANTIC INCOME.

MONEY PLEASES ME, AND I ALLOW MYSELF TO RECEIVE IT.

MY NAME IS_____ AND I AM RICH AND PROSPEROUS.

I FEEL PROSPEROUS EVERY SINGLE DAY.

I ALLOW MY WEALTH TO GROW EXPONENTIALLY THIS YEAR.

I AM AFFLUENT AND JOYFUL.

MY WALLET IS FULL OF CASH!

MY DEBT IS PAID OFF, AND I STILL HAVE LOTS OF MONEY.

I ACCEPT LIFE'S TREASURES WITH GRATITUDE.

**MY LEVEL OF PROSPERITY GROWS EXPONENTIALLY
EVERY DAY. MY ATTITUDE OF GRATITUDE DRAWS
WEALTH AND AFFLUENCE TO ME WITH EASE.**

I LOVE MONEY!

MONEY IS MY FRIEND.

I HAVE A PROSPEROUS INVESTMENT PORTFOLIO.

MY RETIREMENT ACCOUNTS ARE A BOUNTY OF WEALTH FOR ME.

**MY MONEY ENHANCES MY LIFE AND THE LIFE OF
THOSE AROUND ME IN A BALANCED MANNER.**

I TRUST MYSELF WITH INFINITE WEALTH.

**I GRATEFULLY ACCEPT MY STATUS AS A
WEALTHY, AFFLUENT WOMAN (OR MAN).**

Demeter is here to help you integrate the idea that money is your friend. There's nothing bad about it. You are a person of principle and caring, and by aligning with the goddesses you will use money for good and you can be trusted with it.

After you've compiled your ten statements, sit in a meditative posture with your journal nearby. Close your eyes and say the following out loud, "Thank you, Demeter, for joining me now. I am grateful for your presence and help. I ask that all that we do together be for the very highest good of all life."

Feel Demeter sit across from you. With your journal in your lap, reach out your hands and feel Demeter's spirit hands join with yours. When you're ready, say your ten affirmative statements slowly with feeling, in succession. Demeter will be saying those words with you. Feel and hear yourself say those words of affirmation. Sense and perceive Demeter's voice joining with yours as you speak those words of wealth aloud.

After that is complete, write in your journal about how it felt and anything you noticed. Journal about any emotions that came up or thoughts that popped into your head. Notice how it felt to connect with Demeter. You can ask her to help you with this or any other area of your life. Remember that our guides do not have carte blanche to help us unless we ask. So ask Demeter for help and blessings. She is eager to give them.

It is safe for you to be rich and prosperous. You will use your wealth to enhance your life and the lives of those around you. Let Demeter be your guide and helper on this journey.

PROTECTION AND INTUITION

The following meditation and activity will bring you into a powerful circle of protection and from that safe space enhance and open your intuition.

GODDESS OF PROTECTION MEDITATION

The following meditation will bring you into a circle of protection. The world is generally a safe place. Sometimes we feel fearful or anxious, and sometimes we have real things we need to be aware of to keep ourselves safe. Enter the goddess Durga. Durga is a specialist in keeping you safe, and she is definitely known in the Hindu tradition for kicking butt and taking names. She is a goddess who clears away that which no longer serves so that new growth can occur. She is mother, wise woman, benevolent destroyer, and shepherdess of evolution via rebirth. Allow Durga's courage and psychic strength to be transferred to you and to bring out those qualities in you.

Sit or lie down in a meditative posture. Get comfortable, but in this meditation you will want to stay relatively aware. State out loud or internally, "I ask that all that transpires in the entirety of this meditation be for the very highest good of all life and in accordance with universal natural law. Helping all and harming none. I invite Durga, representative of the Great Goddess, into my life. I accept her protection and blessings for my highest good."

Feel Durga's presence within you. What does it feel like? In a moment, you will use a powerful incantation to protect yourself. You can memorize these words and say them whenever you choose. Durga will help you. You do not need to do a full meditation to use these words of protection. I like to use them before I walk into a crowded space such as an airport or a mall. You can say these words if you feel trepidation about a situation any time you choose.

Say the following either internally in your mind or out loud. Either way works: "I seal and protect all wormholes, portals, doorways, and openings in my physical and etheric bodies. I do this in all dimensions, all interdimensions, and all realities for my highest good and the highest good of all life. It is done."

Whenever you say these words aloud, visualize the area around you as a sphere three feet out from your body. Watch this area become sealed and protected. Visualize it. As you say the words, you can envision that bubble around you strengthening. Or you can envision light coming down around the bubble and sealing it. You can even envision a stream of light spiraling down from above you, from below you, or both and circling around the sphere and sealing and protecting it.

When you have time, meditate with Durga and enact this incantation. Before bed is a great opportunity, but at other times when you do not have time to meditate you can still say these words. You can even write them on a note card and keep it in your purse.

GODDESS OF INTUITION ACTIVITY

This activity will help you open your intuitive senses on every level with gentleness and ease. Intuition and psychic ability are not things that you want to force or push. It is healthier and more holistically balanced to allow these talents to emerge with gradual encouragement. This intuition activity is inspired by Themis, goddess of prophecy. Themis was thought to be the goddess who spoke to the high priestesses who served over many years at the famed Oracle of Delphi in ancient Greece. People would come from far and wide to receive guidance from the goddess Themis and her highly trained initiates, who were powerful medicine women in their own right.

So today you get to do an activity with a renowned and heralded intuitive trainer in the form of a loving, benevolent goddess. What could be better?

One of the first things you will learn from this experience is that beings in nonphysical form are as real as beings in tangible, physical form. One simply exists only in the form of energy, and the other exists in the forms of matter and energy. That's the main difference between you and a spirit guide.

Our goddess friends bring us extra wisdom and healing because they have access to infinite information and energy as a result of their nonphysical status. Themis is now inviting you to tap into this bestowal of goodness. Her contribution today will be to help you open your intuition to a new level. You can do the following activity as frequently as you would like. Once a day is plenty. Or you can do it just one time and you'll still reap benefits from it for days and weeks to come.

Do this in a place where you will be undisturbed for at least the next fifteen minutes. Stand with your feet a little bit more than shoulder width apart. With your hands at your sides, raise your palms up to about waist level. Bring together the tip of your thumb and your middle finger on both hands. While staying in about the same place, spin all the way around to the left three times.

Next, bring together the tips of your thumb, middle finger, and pointer finger. Still in a wide stance, bring the tips of all six fingers up to rest between your eyebrows just above the bridge of your nose. Feel the energy in your hands and brow center pulsing.

Now say out loud, "I activate my pineal gland to open the gateway to my intuitive senses in a way that is balanced, healthy, and for my highest good. I activate my second sight, my clairaudience, my clairsentience, my claircognizance, my sense of psychic smell, my sense of psychic touch, and my sense of psychic taste. I invite Themis to take my hand and guide me through life and in all ways. I receive her blessings with gratitude and allow her to enhance and open my intuitive senses for my highest good."

Now lie down on your back in a comfortable place nearby for a few minutes. Feel the goddess Themis within you and allow yourself to be open to whatever happens. Your various psychic senses will be activating and opening, and so you just need to rest and allow. You may sense colors or images, sounds or smells, feel feelings or think new thoughts. Simply observe the process as a witness and allow it to unfold without trying to influence it in any way. After about ten to twenty minutes, when that feels complete, you can return to daily life. Make sure to drink plenty of water and give yourself some time to come back into full physical presence. Make sure to keep a journal near your bed at night and start writing down your dreams. They are going to be enhanced with lots of intuitive information and healing. Have fun!

HAPPINESS AND CONFIDENCE

The following meditation and activity will fill you with happiness and confidence with the help of joyful, powerful goddesses. Yay!

GODDESS OF HAPPINESS MEDITATION

This next meditation is designed to help you connect with happiness and joy. There are so many forms of happiness, and you have the amazing opportunity in this life to try them all out and see which your favorites are. Choosing joy is a conscious choice every day. Joy is the highest vibration in the known universe, and when we feel happiness and joy, we have the ability to heal more easily and deeply.

Our guide into the land of happiness today will be the shining Shinto goddess Uzume from Japan. She is a revered goddess of happiness and is known for her dancing.

Get comfortable and relaxed in a cozy spot on the couch or bed. Keep your journal nearby to jot down any notes. Close your eyes and bring your awareness to the center of your chest. Notice how it feels there. Notice any pulsing or tingling or warmth. Notice how you're feeling emotionally. If you had to give the emotion you are currently feeling a name, what would it be? There's no wrong or right or good or bad answer. Notice what comes up.

Now, internally or out loud, repeat the following: "I make a conscious commitment to choose joy in each moment. I make choices that promote my happiness, and I acknowledge that I deserve happiness. I am worthy of joy. I connect with Uzume in joyful gratitude. I invite her to infuse my life with happiness. I accept her benevolent blessings in all areas of my life. I ask Uzume to guide me and give her clearance to intervene on my behalf to make my life more joyful and harmonious and to help me live my heart's desires."

Place one hand or both hands on the center of your chest. Notice again how you feel. Now repeat the following affirmative statement mantra over and over in your mind or out loud: "I am joy." Keep saying it aloud and allow yourself to feel it. Keep repeating the mantra "I am joy" as you picture bright white sparkling light radiating through your body. Notice the direction from which it is coming. Does it come from above you? Does it come from all around you? Does it come from within you under your hand in the center of your chest? Is it expanding from your center outward? Or all of the above?

Feel Uzume come closer. She extends her hands to you, and you can reach your hand out to her. Hold hands with her and with the essence of happiness. What does this goddess evoke in you? As you hold hands with her, allow yourself to receive any healing and guidance that she has to offer. You can say yes to her to let her know that you are open to receiving anything for your highest good. Make sure you tell her "Thank you."

As you return to your day, bring the essence of joy with you. Throughout your day you can repeat the statement "I am joy" to infuse that moment with the essence of happiness.

GODDESS OF CONFIDENCE ACTIVITY

This activity is about fostering your confidence and enhancing your sense of self-worth. It's important that we actively work on empowering ourselves if we want to live a happy, accomplished, healthy life. Navigating today's society requires self-confidence. It requires an ability to face fear and banish self-doubt even in the face of uncertainty. Your confidence is contagious, and you can empower other women and people who are living from their hearts to lead with courage. It is courageous to face your fears. You will find victory in your vulnerability while allowing yourself to be guided by the divine feminine within you. Our representative of the Great Goddess to assist us with confidence is Inanna.

Inanna is a courageous and powerful goddess. When her sister, Ereshkigal, captured her lover and dismembered him, scattering his pieces throughout the underworld, Inanna faced her fears and rescued him. She descended through seven gates into the underworld. At each gate, she had to face an aspect of herself. She was facing her shadow. She had to look her fear in the face and do it anyway. She had to face her vulnerability to be triumphant. And triumph she did, for Inanna retrieved all the pieces of her beloved, Dumuzi, and reassembled him, reconstituting him back into his original form as a representation of the Divine Masculine. Being confident does not mean that you don't doubt yourself or feel apprehensive. It means you feel the fear and do it anyway. That is the extraordinary stuff of which leaders are made.

Gather this book, your journal, and a candle. Go into a room where you have a mirror and can dim or turn out the lights. An interior bathroom is a great option. Light and set up your candle in a spot where it will be safe to let it burn unsupervised. Have the candle close enough to illuminate the area where you will stand in front of the mirror. Keep your journal on hand.

Turn off the lights so that the only illumination is the candle. You should still be able to see the words in the book. If you can't, grab a couple more candles.

Now, with the candle's light, take a few minutes to look at yourself in the mirror. Look at your face. Do this with no judgments, just neutral acceptance. When you are ready, say the following aloud: "I ask that all that transpires in the entirety of this mirror-gazing session be for the very highest good of all life and in accordance with universal natural law, helping all and harming none. I now connect with Inanna and all of my highest vibrational goddess guides. I ask Inanna to guide me and help me cultivate confidence so that I can achieve my goals and experience my heart's desires with joy."

Gaze into your own eyes with soft focus and allow them to unfocus and relax. Take a look deep within yourself. The flickering light from the candles may help you see different parts of yourself. You may see faces in your face. Your face may change in the mirror ever so slightly. You may see the face of Ishtar flash in the mirror. Or you may see other goddesses in your own reflection. Yes, these are separate beings, but they are also reflections of yourself. You are the Divine Feminine.

As you gaze into your own eyes and face, you may see aspects of yourself from other times: past, present, and future. Simply allow this to unfold. Grasp at nothing. Remain unattached and simply observe. Let go of your identity and feel the interconnection of all time and space. Understand that although you are currently existing in duality, which is where the dimensions of time and space intersect, many nonphysical beings exist outside of time and space that you can access anywhere and anytime. Your higher self exists within you right now, in this time and this space. It also exists in eternity and throughout all existence and beyond.

While feeling your eternal nature and gazing into your face in the flickering light, repeat the following affirmative statements out loud: "I own my space. I am present in my body. I make decisions with ease and trust myself. I speak my truth in a way that is well received and aligned with my heart's desires. I feel confident. I know that I am worthy of good things. My choices are healthy and holistically good for me and the world. My self-esteem is healthy, and I feel good. I feel self-assured, and I know that I can rely on myself to create the life I choose."

Even if those statements do not all feel true, you can fake it till you make it. Speak to yourself with confidence and caring. You are the architect of your life. Make healthy choices and take decisive action to create the life you desire. You have that power. You are not a victim of circumstances. You are a creator with an opportunity to craft a joyous existence of your choosing.

CONCLUSION

An infinite benevolent pantheon of goddesses is available to assist you in every moment. This book has introduced you to just a small percentage of the many goddesses with whom humans have connected over the existence of the human race.

You might wonder why goddesses would want to help you. It is because they are planetary healers. They love each and every one of us and all life, for that matter. Goddesses are archetypal energies personified. They are helpers, healers, midwives of our dreams, caring friends to lend an ear, benevolent protectors, teachers, and much more.

I hope that during our journey together in this book you have connected with the goddesses that surround you and especially with the goddess within you. You are an incarnation of the Divine Feminine. *You* are the goddess. You can harness this power and presence within you at any time you choose. You can use it to better your life and your world. Go forth and share the compassion, caring, and innovative ideas of the Great Goddess. You matter. You are a crucial piece of the puzzle that continues the journey of evolution on our planet. Deep within you, find that little bit of goddess.

GODDESS COMMUNITY

One of the ingredients in much of the healing and connection we had to the goddess in the past was community. We gathered in groups whether in the red tent, in tribal circles, in a ritual to help the village, or as educated priestesses and goddess temples. We had a sisterhood on which to lean and with which to share. It's crucial that we cultivate this again. Each woman in our lives is a reflection of the Divine Feminine. And when we gather, amazing things happen. I've collected some resources for you here, but I also urge you to get out and find your tribe. I found part of my tribe in dance fitness. I found part of my tribe in my soul sister author colleagues. I am fortunate enough to have found part of my tribe in middle school and high school in the form of amazing friends. Soul sisters are all around! It is our job as goddesses in training to recognize one another and embrace one another with acceptance and support.

Goddess Books

Speaking of soul sisters, my amazing author sister Emma Mildon wrote a beautiful book called *Evolution of Goddess*.

My all-time favorite goddess book is *The Moon under Her Feet* by Clysta Kinstler. Another engaging goddess book is *The Red Tent* by Anita Diamant.

Also, *I Remember Union: The Story of Mary Magdalena* by Flo Aeveia Magdalena and Jayn Stewart, and *The Woman of Wyrrd: The Arousal of the Inner Fire, Jaguar Woman, Windhorse Woman,* and *Shakkai:*

Woman of the Sacred Garden by Lynn V. Andrews are all excellent.

Some of my favorite Celtic goddess–based historical fiction includes several books by Marion Zimmer Bradley: *The Mists of Avalon*, *The Forest House*, *Lady of Avalon*, and *Priestess of Avalon*.

The following sources will help you find information on specific goddesses:

Illustrated Dictionary of Mythology

Philip Wilkinson, *Illustrated Dictionary of Mythology* (New York, DK Publishing, 2006), 10–123:

ADITI—Mother of the gods and the cosmos; Hindu/India

AMATERASU—Sun goddess and weaving; Shinto/Japan

AMMUT—Devourer of the dead; ate the hearts of the wicked; Egyptian/Egypt

APHRODITE—Goddess of love and beauty; Greek/Ancient Greece

ARTEMIS—Goddess of hunting, chastity, and maidenhood; Greek/Ancient Greece

ASHERAT—Fertility goddess; Canaanite/Mediterranean coast

ATHENA—Goddess of wisdom, weaving, and warrior skills; Greek/Ancient Greece, animal: owl

BABA YAGA—Goddess of death; Slavic/Eastern Europe

BASTET—Goddess of sexuality and childbirth; Egyptian/Egypt; animal: cat

BENTEN (BENZAI-TEN)—Goddess of music, luck, and expressiveness; Shinto/Japan; symbol: biwa

BENZAITEN—Goddess of love; Hindu/India

BRIGHT CLOUD WOMAN—Protector of fishes; Native tradition/American West Coast

BUFFALO WOMAN—Caused buffalo herds to scatter; Native tradition/American Great Plains

CALYPSO—Goddess of silence; Greek/Ancient Greece

CHALCHIUHTLICUE—Goddess of rivers, lakes, and springs, also seen as a goddess of childbirth (water breaking); Aztec/Central America

CHASKA-QOYLOR (VENUS)—A star deity, sun's handmaiden, patron of young girls; Incan/Central America

CHANGING WOMAN—creator goddess, represents the life cycle; Navaho/Southwest America

CHICOMECOATL—Corn goddess, represented stored seeds for the next year's harvest; Aztec/Central America

CINTEOTL—Corn goddess; Aztec/Central America

CORN WOMAN—Made corn grow; Native tradition/American Great Plains

COYOLXAUHQUI—Goddess of the moon; Aztec/Central America

CYBELE—Great Mother or mother of the gods; Roman/Roman Empire

DEMETER—Goddess of the harvest; Greek/Ancient Greece; symbol: a head of grain

DEVI—(Mahadevi) femininity; Hindu/India

DUGNAI—Household goddess, helped in breadmaking; Slavic/Eastern Europe

DURGA—Warrior goddess; Hindu/India

EPONA—Goddess of the earth; Celtic/Britain and Western Europe; animal: horse

ERESHKIGAL—Goddess of darkness, ruler of the underworld; Babylonian/Western Asia; creature: part vulture, part snake

ERIS—Soddess of chaos; Greek/Ancient Greece; symbol: golden apple

FIRST MOTHER—Sacrificed herself for her people during famine; Native tradition/Eastern North America

FLORA—Goddess of spring and nature; Roman/Roman Empire

FORTUNA—Goddess of chance; Roman/Roman Empire; symbols: rudder, wheel, and cornucopia

FREYJA—Fertility goddess, magic and riches; Norse/Scandinavia; symbol of sexual freedom

FRIGG—Goddess of the rain and fertility, seer of the future, queen of Asgard; Norse/Scandinavia

GANGA—Represents the Ganges, purity; Hindu/India

GEFION—Attendant to Frigg; Norse/Scandinavia

GIRL WITHOUT PARENTS—First living being, helped to create the world; Apache/Southwest America

GREAT GODDESS, THE (MOTHER EARTH)—Creator of the universe, guardian of fruitfulness, antiquity

GUINEVERE—King Arthur's queen; Celtic/Britain and Western Europe

HANNAHANNA—Mother goddess, Hittite; Anatolian/Western Asia

HARMONIA—Goddess of harmony; Greek/Ancient Greece

HATHOR—Cow goddess, guardian of women and protector of lovers; Egyptian/Egypt, plant: papyrus

HAUMEA—Goddess of childbirth; Hawaiian/Hawaii

HEBE—Goddess of youth, presided over serving ambrosia and nectar; Greek/Ancient Greece

HECATE—Goddess of magic, patron of witches; Greek/Ancient Greece

HERA—Goddess of marriage and childbirth; queen of Olympus, Greek/Ancient Greece

HESTIA—Goddess of the hearth, overseer of social order; Greek/Ancient Greece

HINA—Great Goddess of the Polynesians; Polynesian/Pacific Islands

HINE-NUI-TE-PO—Goddess of death, giantess; Maori/New Zealand

HINE-TEI-WAUIN—Goddess of childbirth; Polynesian/Pacific Islands, spell is recited to make birthing easier (still practiced in New Zealand)

HSI WANG MU (QUEEN MOTHER WANG)—Goddess of eternal life, patron of women; Chinese/China, reason to connect: when a daughter is born

HYGEIA—Health goddess; Greek/Ancient Greece

IDUN—Spring goddess; Norse/Scandinavia; symbol: apples of youth

IRIS—Goddess of rainbows, messenger of the gods; Greek/Ancient Greece

ISHTAR—Fertility and sexual love goddess, Star of the Evening, identified with the planet Venus; Babylonian/Western Asia; sacred animal: lion. In the Sumerian form, she was the goddess of war and the Star of the Morning

ISIS—Birthed sun/moon, heaven/earth, female/male, divine wisdom, created the Nile; Egyptian/Egypt

IXCHEL—Lady Rainbow, goddess of all things and pregnancy, could foretell the future; Mayan/Central America

KAMRUSEPA—Goddess of healing and magic; Hittite, Anatolian/Western Asia

KI—Earth goddess; mother of the gods and mortals; Sumerian/Western Asia,

KIKIMORA—Household goddess, aided hardworking women; Slavic/Eastern Europe

KUAN YIN—Goddess of mercy, healer; Buddhist/India and China; connect with to receive help in conception

KYLLIKI—Love goddess; Finnish/Northern Europe

LADY OF THE LAKE—Protector of humanity; Celtic/Britain and Western Europe

LAKSHMI—Goddess of good fortune and beauty, Hindu/India

LUONNOTAR—Creator of the world; Finnish/Northern Europe

MA'AT—Goddess of truth, harmony, and justice; Egyptian/Egypt

MAMA KILYA—Goddess of the moon, passing time, and fertility, also protector of women; Incan/South America; symbol: eclipses

MAWU—Goddess of the moon; Fon/Western Africa

MATI-SYRA-ZEMLYA—Earth goddess; Slavic/Eastern Europe

MESKHENET—Goddess of childbirth; Egyptian/Egypt; symbol: birthing tile

MORGAN LE FAY—Fairy, Celtic/; Britain and Western Europe

MORRIGAN—Goddess of war, sexuality; Celtic/Ireland; animal: raven

MUT—Goddess of the sky, surrogate royal mother; Egyptian/Egypt, animal: cat or cow

NAMMU—Primeval sea, birthed the sky and earth; Sumerian/Western Asia

NANTOSUELTA—Goddess of hearth and home, water goddess; Celtic/Britain and Western Europe

NEITH—Mother goddess, invented childbirth; Egyptian/Nile Delta and Egypt; symbol: shield with two crossed arrows

NEPHTHYS—Funerary goddess; Egyptian/Egypt

NINHURSAG—Earth mother; Sumerian/Western Asia

NINLIL—Fertility goddess; Mesopotamian/Western Asia

NINMAH—Goddess of birth; Mesopotamian/Western Asia, created humans

NU WA—Creator goddess, fertility; Chinese/China, animal: snake

NUT—Goddess of the sky; Egyptian/Egypt

PACHA MAMA—Earth goddess, giver of life; Incan/South America; common offerings: llamas and coca leaves

PAPA—Mother Earth; Maori/New Zealand

PELE—Fire goddess, hula; Hawaiian/Hawaii

PERSEPHONE—Goddess of spring, fertility; Greek/Ancient Greece

PINGA (PANA)—hunting goddess; Inuit/Arctic region

RENENET—Cobra goddess, leads the harvest and guardian of the pharaoh; can help with crop growth, prosperity, and food abundance; Egyptian/Egypt

SARASVATI—Mother of the arts and language; Hindu/India, invented Sanskrit

SATI—Ideal of feminine love, Hindu/India; reincarnated into Parvati

SEA WOMAN (SEDNA)—Mother of sea beasts, protector of sea creatures; Inuit/Arctic region

SEKHMET—Punishment goddess, Egyptian/Egypt; represented with a lion's head on a woman's body

SELENE—Goddess of the moon; Greek/Ancient Greece

SERKET—Scorpion goddess, has powers to repel evil and involved in funeral rites; Egyptian/Egypt

SESHAT—Queen of the library, scribe to the gods; Egyptian/Egypt

SHAPASH—Goddess of the sun, torch of the gods; Canaanite/Mediterranean coast

SIF—Wife of Thor; Norse/Scandinavia

SPIDER WOMAN—Brings good fortune; Hopi/Southwest America

STORM GODDESS—Can create floods; Mayan/Central America

TAWERET—Protector of women in childbirth; Egyptian/Egypt; ways to connect: wear a charm of Taweret or place mother's milk in vase and perform a good luck spell

TEFNUT—Goddess of moisture; Egyptian/Egypt; animal forms: serpent and lioness, represented by pair of splitting lips

THEMIS—Goddess of justice, known for wise and just advice; Greek/Ancient Greece

TRIPLE MOTHER—carrying a dog, a fish, and a basket of fruit; Celtic/Britain and Western Europe

USHAS—Dawn goddess, reborn every morning; Hindu/ India

UZUME—Goddess of happiness, dancing deity; Shinto/Japan

VENUS—Goddess of love; Roman/Roman Empire

VESTA—Goddess of the hearth; Roman/Roman Empire

XOCHIQUETZAL—Goddess of flowers and fruit, also goddess of music and ruler of part of the underworld; Aztec/Central America

YELLOW CORN GIRL—Along with her twin brother brought corn to the Navaho; Navaho/Southwest America; corn is a sacred plant in ceremonies

YEWA—First woman in existence; Fon/Western Africa

YORUBA—Goddess of the earth, fertility deity; Yoruba people/Nigeria and Western Africa

WAKAHIRU-ME—Goddess of the rising sun; Shinto/Japan

WAGALAK SISTERS—Named wildlife, plants, and places as they traveled; Yolngu people/Australia

The Book of Goddesses

Kris Waldherr, *The Book of Goddesses* (Hillsboro, OR: Beyond Words, 1995):

CHANG-O/CHANG-E—Moon goddess, associated with moon cakes; ancient China

DIANA—Mother of wildlife and moon goddess; Roman/Roman Empire

GWENHWYFAR—First lady of Wales; Welsh/Britain

INANNA—Queen of heaven, goddess of rain and moonlight; Sumerian/Iraq and Sumer, Bronze Age

JUNO—Goddess of all, patron of marriage and women; Roman/Roman Empire

LAKSHMI—Attracted to sparkling jewels; people use lanterns

MAIA—Star goddess, also of spring and rebirth; Greek/Greece

NYAI RORO KIDUL—Mermaid goddess of the South Seas; Javanese/Java

OYA—Ruler of the Niger River, patron of female leadership and eloquence; Yoruba people/ Nigeria; connect through long maroon bead necklace

SARASVATI—Goddess of all knowledge; Hindu/India

TARA—Mother goddess, protector, first female Buddha; Tibetan Buddhism/Tibet

UKEMOCHI—Goddess of food; Shinto/Japan

YEMANA—Goddess of the ocean; Santeria/Cuba; to connect: wear seven silver bracelets (or ones with blue and white beads)

ZORYA—Trinity of goddesses, represent dawn/twilight/midnight, guardians of the universe; Russian mythology/Russia

Goddesses: Knowledge Cards

Susan Seddon Boulet and Michael Babcock, *Goddesses: Knowledge Cards* (Portland, OR: Pomegranate; cards edition, 2003):

KORE—Blessed Death; holds the keys to lower and heavenly worlds; pre-Greek

QUEEN OF HEAVEN (VIRGIN MARY)—Mystery and sacredness of birth

Power of Flower Cards

Isha Lerner, *Power of Flower Cards* (Stamford, CT: U.S. Games Systems, 2014):

ASTARTE—True sovereign of the world, mother of all star-children; pre-Christianity; apple blossom

EVE—Christianity; all living things

VENUS OF WILLENDORF—Self-impregnation; productivity and beauty; Paleolithic

Goddess Guidance Oracle Cards

Doreen Virtue. *Goddess Guidance Oracle Cards* (Carlsbad, CA: Hay House, 2002):

ABUNDANTIA—Roman/Norse; prosperity, success, abundance, good fortune

AERACURA—Celtic/Germanic

KALI—Pure female energy, protector of the universe, womb

Africana: The Encyclopedia of the African and African American Experience

"Iemanjá." *Africana: The Encyclopedia of the African and African American Experience* (2nd ed.)

(New York: Oxford African American Studies Center, 2008):

JANAÍNA—Also known as Yemanja, goddess of the ocean; Yoruba/Brazil

The Origins of the Guadalupe Tradition in Mexico

Timothy Matovina. "The Origins of the Guadalupe Tradition in Mexico." *Catholic Historical Review*, vol. 100, no. 2, Spring 2014, 243–270:

> **OUR LADY OF CHARITY**—Cuba
>
> **OUR LADY OF REMEDIES**—Spain
>
> **QUEEN OF CUBA/COPPER**—Cuba

"Why the Iconic Virgin of Charity Means So Much to Cubans and Pope Francis"

"Why the Iconic Virgin of Charity Means So Much to Cubans and Pope Francis," *Washington Post*, Sept. 22, 2015:

LILITH—Goddess of death, Hebrew

OUR LADY OF CHARITY (VIRGIN OF CHARITY OF EL COBRE)—Catholic, provides hope and salvation, Cuba, copper, flower: sunflower

SHAKTI—Feminine energy, force that created goddesses

BIBLIOGRAPHY

Ackerman, Susan. *Gender and Difference in Ancient Israel* (Minneapolis: Fortress Press, 2006).

Adler, Margot. *Drawing Down the Moon: Witches, Druids, Goddess-Worshippers, and Other Pagans in America Today, revised and expanded edition* (New York: Beacon Press, 1986).

Alvar, Jaime. *Romanising Oriental Gods: Myth, Salvation, and Ethics in the Cults of Cybele, Isis, and Mithras* (Boston: Brill, 2008).

Baan, Natalie. "Virgin Mother Crone: Myths and Mysteries of the Triple Goddess." *Parabola* 19, no. 2 (1994). *Academic OneFile*. Accessed March 1, 2019, http://link.gale-group.com.ezproxy.fgcu.edu/apps/doc/A15256411/AONE?u=gale15690&sid=AONE&xid=c222c7c9.

Black, Jeremy, and Anthony Green. *Gods, Demons and Symbols of Ancient Mesopotamia: An Illustrated Dictionary* (London: British Museum Press, 1992).

Boyce, Mary. "Anāhīd," *Encyclopædia Iranica*. Accessed Mar ch 9, 2019, http://www.iranicaonline.org/articles/anahid.

Campbell, Joseph. *Goddesses: Mysteries of the Divine Feminine* (Novato, CA: Joseph Campbell Foundation, 2013).

Cochrane, Ev. *The Many Faces of Venus: The Planet Venus in Ancient Myth and Religion* (Ames, IA: Aeon Publishing, 1997).

Conway, D. J. *Maiden, Mother, Crone: The Myth and Reality of the Triple Goddess* (Woodbury, MN: Llewellyn Publications, 1994).

De Franceschini, M., & Veneziano, G. (2013). "Architecture and Archaeoastronomy in Hadrian's Villa Near Tivoli, Rome." *Nexus Network Journal, 15*(3), 457–485, doi:http://dx.doi.org.ezproxy.fgcu.edu/10.1007/s00004-013-0161-9.

Editors of Encyclopedia Britannica, "Astarte," *Encyclopedia Britannica*. Accessed March 6, 2019, https://www.britannica.com/topic/Astarte.

Fontenrose, Joseph. *Python: A Study of Delphic Myth and Its Origins* (Berkeley: University of California Press, 1959).

"goddess, n.1." OED Online. December 2018. Oxford University Press. Accessed January 11, 2019, http://www.oed.com/viewdictionaryentry/Entry/11125.

Harding, M. Esther. *Woman's Mysteries: Ancient and Modern* (Boston: Shambhala, 1971).

Hinke, W. J. *A New Boundary Stone of Nebuchadrezzar I from Nippur with a Concordance of Proper Names and a Glossary of the Kudurru Inscriptions Thus Far Published* (Philadelphia: University of Pennsylvania, 1907).

Kinstler, Clysta. *The Moon Under Her Feet*. (San Francisco: HarperSanFrancisco, 1991).

Kraemer, Ross Shepard. *Her Share of the Blessings: Women's Religions Among Pagans, Jews, and Christians in the Greco-Roman World* (New York: Oxford University Press, 1992), http://search.ebscohost.com/login.aspx?direct=true&db=nlebk&AN=52741&site=e host-live.

Littleton, C. Scott. "The Pneuma Enthusiastikon: On the Possibility of Hallucinogenic 'Vapors' at Delphi and Dodona." *Ethos* 14, no. 1 (1986): 76–91, http://www.jstor.org. ezproxy.fgcu.edu/stable/639992.

Lochtefeld, James G. *The Illustrated Encyclopedia of Hinduism: A–M* (New York: Rosen Publishing Group, 2002).

Maupin, Kathy. *The Secret Female Hormone* (New York: Hay House, 2015).

McNamee, Gregory. "Solstice vs. Equinox." *Virginia Quarterly Review* 90, no. 3 (2014): 205. *Academic OneFile.* Accessed March 1, 2019, http://link.galegroup.com.ezproxy. fgcu.edu/apps/doc/A388189757/AONE?u=gale15690&sid=AONE&xid=29e6401a.

Mildon, Emma. *Evolution of the Goddess* (New York: Enliven Books/Atria, 2018).

Patai, Raphael. *The Hebrew Goddess* (Detroit: Wayne State University Press, 1990).

Rufus, Anneli, and Lawson, Kristan. *Goddess Sites: Europe* (New York: HarperCollins, 1991).

Sermon, R. (2000). "The Celtic Calendar and the English Year." *Mankind Quarterly, 40*(4), 401–420. Retrieved from http://ezproxy.fgcu.edu/login?url=https://search-proquest-com.ezproxy.fgcu.edu/docview/222467227?accountid=10919.

Shadrach, Nineveh. *Codex of Love: Reflections from the Heart of Ishtar* (New York: Ishtar Publishing, 2005).

Stone, Merlin. *When God Was a Woman* (New York: Mariner Books, 1978).

Trevarthen, Geo Athena. "The Celtic Origins of Halloween Transcend Fear." *Phi Kappa Phi Forum* 90, no. 3 (2010). *Academic OneFile.* Accessed March 1, 2019, http://link.galegroup. com/apps/doc/A239169935/AONE?u=10002_ccpl&sid=AONE&xid=0ad98633.

Wilkinson, Philip. *Illustrated Dictionary of Mythology* (New York, DK Publishing, 2006).

Williams, George M. *Handbook of Hindu Mythology* (New York: Oxford University Press, 2008).

Wilson, Robert A. *Ishtar Rising: Or, Why the Goddess Went to Hell and What to Expect Now That She's Returning* (New York: New Falcon Publications, 1988).

ENDNOTES

History of the Divine Feminine

"Men, in fact, had very limited . . ."—D. J. Conway. *Maiden, Mother, Crone: The Myth and Reality of the Triple Goddess* (Woodbury, MN: Llewellyn Publications, 1994), 11.

"The earliest calculations of goddess worship . . ."—M. Esther Harding. *Woman's Mysteries: Ancient and Modern* (Boston: Shambhala, 1971).

"These early societies also modeled . . ."—D. J. Conway. *Maiden, Mother, Crone: The Myth and Reality of the Triple Goddess* (Woodbury, MN: Llewellyn Publications, 1994), 12.

"The subsequent Neolithic era produced some . . ."—D. J. Conway. *Maiden, Mother, Crone: The Myth and Reality of the Triple Goddess* (Woodbury, MN: Llewellyn Publications, 1994), 13.

"This period is also interesting in that it . . ."—Joseph Campbell. *Goddesses: Mysteries of the Divine Feminine* (Novato, CA: Joseph Campbell Foundation, 2013), 3–6.

"Possibly as a result, the images . . ."—D. J. Conway. *Maiden, Mother, Crone: The Myth and Reality of the Triple Goddess* (Woodbury, MN: Llewellyn Publications, 1994), 12.

"This shows the functionality and structure . . ."—D. J. Conway, *Maiden, Mother, Crone: The Myth and Reality of the Triple Goddess* (Woodbury, MN: Llewellyn Publications, 1994), 11.

"These figurines emphasize . . ."—Joseph Campbell. *Goddesses: Mysteries of the Divine Feminine* (Novato, CA: Joseph Campbell Foundation, 2013), 7–8.

"The word goddess itself starts . . ."—*Oxford English Dictionary,* online edition (Oxford: Oxford University Press, 2018), "goddess, n.1," http://www.oed.com/viewdictionaryentry/Entry/11125.

"What was once limited to strictly . . ."—Joseph Campbell. *Goddesses: Mysteries of the Divine Feminine* (Novato, CA: Joseph Campbell Foundation, 2013), 16–17.

"This continued to sustain . . ."—Joseph Campbell. *Goddesses: Mysteries of the Divine Feminine* (Novato, CA: Joseph Campbell Foundation, 2013), 5–6.

"Temples have been around since . . ."—Joseph Campbell. *Goddesses: Mysteries of the Divine Feminine* (Novato, CA: Joseph Campbell Foundation, 2013), 5.

"A female high priestess known . . ."—C. Scott Littleton. "The Pneuma Enthusiastikon: On the Possibility of Hallucinogenic 'Vapors' at Delphi and Dodona," *Ethos 14*, no. 1 (1986): 76–91, http://www.jstor.org.ezproxy.fgcu.edu/stable/639992.

"That prophetic trance is popularly . . ."—"*The Pneuma Enthusiastikon: On the Possibility of Hallucinogenic 'Vapors' at Delphi and Dodona,*" *Ethos 14*, no. 1 (1986): 76–91, http://www.jstor.org.ezproxy.fgcu.edu/stable/639992.

"However, research has shown that . . ."—Joseph Fontenrose. *Python: A Study of Delphic Myth and Its Origins* (Berkeley: University of California Press, 1959).

"Matriarchal societies provided so many . . ." D. J. Conway. *Maiden, Mother, Crone: The Myth and Reality of the Triple Goddess* (Woodbury, MN: Llewellyn Publications, 1994), 13–14.

"Given the nature of female-oriented . . ."—D. J. Conway. *Maiden, Mother, Crone: The Myth and Reality of the Triple Goddess* (Woodbury, MN: Llewellyn Publications, 1994), 14.

Seasonal Celebrations of the Goddesses

"The spring equinox takes place . . ."—Gregory McNamee. "Solstice vs. Equinox." *Virginia Quarterly Review 90*, no. 3 (2014): 205. *Academic OneFile.*

"In fact, the word Easter is . . ."—Ross Shepard Kraemer. *Her Share of the Blessings: Women's Religions among Pagans, Jews, and Christians in the Greco-Roman World.* (New York: Oxford University Press, 1992).

"The tradition of Beltane, or May Day, comes . . ."—R. Sermon. "The Celtic Calendar and the English Year." *Mankind Quarterly, 40*(4) (2000), 401–420.

"It symbolizes the coming of summer . . ."—R. Sermon. (2000). "About Beltane Fire Festival: What Is Beltane?" Beltane.org. Accessed March 1, 2019, https://beltane.org/about/about-beltane/.

"Celebrated throughout Scotland and Ireland . . ."—R. Sermon (2000). "About Beltane Fire Festival: What Is Beltane?" Beltane.org. Accessed March 1, 2019, https://beltane.org/about/about-beltane/.

"May bushes, which were normally . . ."—R. Sermon (2000). "About Beltane Fire Festival: What Is Beltane?" Beltane.org. Accessed March 1, 2019, https://beltane.org/about/about-beltane/.

"The summer solstice is recognized . . ."—Gregory McNamee. "Solstice vs. Equinox." *Virginia Quarterly Review 90*, no. 3 (2014): 205. Academic OneFile.

"Autumn is another transitional point . . ."—Gregory McNamee. "Solstice vs. Equinox." *Virginia Quarterly Review 90*, no. 3 (2014): 205. Academic OneFile.

"Samhain comes halfway between . . ."—Geo Athena Trevarthen. "The Celtic Origins of Halloween Transcend Fear." *Phi Kappa Phi Forum 90*, no. 3 (2010). Academic OneFile.

"It typically starts on . . ."— Geo Athena Trevarthen. "The Celtic Origins of Halloween Transcend Fear." *Phi Kappa Phi Forum 90*, no. 3 (2010). Academic OneFile.

"Halloween actually has its origin . . ."—Geo Athena Trevarthen. "The Celtic Origins of Halloween Transcend Fear." *Phi Kappa Phi Forum 90*, no. 3 (2010). Academic OneFile.

"Interestingly, for this holiday . . ."— Geo Athena Trevarthen. "The Celtic Origins of Halloween Transcend Fear." *Phi Kappa Phi Forum 90*, no. 3 (2010). Academic OneFile.

"Samhain realizes that cycle that . . ."— Geo Athena Trevarthen. "The Celtic Origins of Halloween Transcend Fear." *Phi Kappa Phi Forum 90*, no. 3 (2010). Academic OneFile.

"The study of mythology . . ."—H. R. Ellis Davidson. *God and Myths of Northern Europe* (New York: Penguin Books, 1990).

Maiden, Mother, Wise Woman

"It is believed that European pantheons observed . . ."—M. Esther Harding. *Woman's Mysteries: Ancient and Modern* (Boston: Shambhala, 1971).

"In the original model of . . ."—Natalie Baan. "Virgin Mother Crone: Myths and Mysteries of the Triple Goddess." *Parabola* 19, no. 2 (1994). Academic OneFile. Accessed March 1, 2019, http://link.galegroup.com.ezproxy.fgcu.edu/apps/doc/A15256411/AONE?u=gale15690&sid=AONE&xid=c222c7c9.

"She is the beginning of life . . ."—D. J. Conway. *Maiden, Mother, Crone: The Myth and Reality of the Triple Goddess* (Woodbury, MN: Llewellyn Publications, 1994), 21.

"Referring back to when the aspects . . ."—D. J. Conway. *Maiden, Mother, Crone: The Myth and Reality of the Triple Goddess* (Woodbury, MN: Llewellyn Publications, 1994), 23.

"The Maiden aspect is curious . . ."—D. J. Conway. *Maiden, Mother, Crone: The Myth and Reality of the Triple Goddess* (Woodbury, MN: Llewellyn Publications, 1994), 24.

"As is often the case with youth, the Maiden . . ."—D. J. Conway. *Maiden, Mother, Crone: The Myth and Reality of the Triple Goddess* (Woodbury, MN: Llewellyn Publications, 1994), 22.

"Another name by which the Maiden . . ."—D. J. Conway. *Maiden, Mother, Crone: The Myth and Reality of the Triple Goddess* (Woodbury, MN: Llewellyn Publications, 1994), 22.

"She is a protectress of the . . ."—D. J. Conway. *Maiden, Mother, Crone: The Myth and Reality of the Triple Goddess* (Woodbury, MN: Llewellyn Publications, 1994), 32.

"An all-female priesthood of nineteen . . ."—Anneli Rufus and Kristan Lawson. *Goddess Sites: Europe* (New York: HarperCollins, 1991).

"In her characterization, she is . . ."—D. J. Conway. *Maiden, Mother, Crone: The Myth and Reality of the Triple Goddess* (Woodbury, MN: Llewellyn Publications, 1994), 33.

"She is associated with the . . ."—D. J. Conway. *Maiden, Mother, Crone: The Myth and Reality of the Triple Goddess* (Woodbury, MN: Llewellyn Publications, 1994), 36.

"This aspect of the Triple Goddess . . ."—D. J. Conway. *Maiden, Mother, Crone: The Myth and Reality of the Triple Goddess* (Woodbury, MN: Llewellyn Publications, 1994), 5.

Evolution of the Evening Star

"You will find it on numerous . . ."—W. J. Hinke. *A New Boundary Stone of Nebuchadrezzar I from Nippur with a Concordance of Proper Names and a Glossary of the Kudurru Inscriptions Thus Far Published* (Philadelphia: University of Pennsylvania, 1907).

"Anahita was the Persian goddess . . ."—Mary Boyce. "Anāhīd." *Encyclopædia Iranica.* Accessed March 9, 2019, http://www.iranicaonline.org/articles/anahid.

"Lakshmi is associated with the . . ."—George M. Williams. *Handbook of Hindu Mythology* (New York: Oxford University Press, 2008), 128.

"In her myth, she chose . . ."—James G. Lochtefeld. *The Illustrated Encyclopedia of Hinduism: A–M* (New York: Rosen Publishing Group, 2002).

"Many rituals are still performed in . . ."—James G. Lochtefeld. *The Illustrated Encyclopedia of Hinduism: A–M* (New York: Rosen Publishing Group, 2002).

"Astarte was associated with the . . ."—Editors of Encyclopedia Britannica, "Astarte." *Encyclopedia Britannica.* Accessed March 6, 2019, https://www.britannica.com/topic/Astarte.

"She is a Mesopotamian version . . ."—Merlin Stone. *When God Was a Woman* (New York: Mariner Books, 1978).

"She helps her devotees and . . ."—Merlin Stone. *When God Was a Woman* (New York: Mariner Books, 1978).

"Her sacred flower is the . . ."—Raphael Patai. *The Hebrew Goddess* (Detroit: Wayne State University Press, 1990), 59.

"Inanna was a Mesopotamian (specifically . . ."—Susan Ackerman. *Gender and Difference in Ancient Israel* (Minneapolis: Fortress Press, 2006).

"There was a large temple . . ."—Merlin Stone. *When God Was a Woman* (New York: Mariner Books, 1978).

"Inanna bestowed blessings of love . . ."—Susan Ackerman. *Gender and Difference in Ancient Israel* (Minneapolis: Fortress Press, 2006).

"Occasionally, certain honored priestesses would . . ."—Merlin Stone. *When God Was a Woman* (New York: Mariner Books, 1978).

"To her who appears in . . ."—Ev Cochrane. *The Many Faces of Venus: The Planet Venus in Ancient Myth and Religion* (Ames, IA: Aeon Publishing, 1997).

"Inanna is also known for . . ."—Susan Ackerman. *Gender and Difference in Ancient Israel* (Minneapolis: Fortress Press, 2006).

"Ishtar was a much-loved Babylonian . . ."—Robert A. Wilson. *Ishtar Rising: Or, Why the Goddess Went to Hell and What to Expect Now That She's Returning* (New York: New Falcon Publications, 1988).

"She held forth the tenets . . ."—Robert A. Wilson. *Ishtar Rising: Or, Why the Goddess Went to Hell and What to Expect Now That She's Returning* (New York: New Falcon Publications, 1988).

"She, too, was seen as . . ."—Nineveh Shadrach. *Codex of Love: Reflections from the Heart of Ishtar* (New York: Ishtar Publishing, 2005).

"Along with her consort, Tammuz . . ."—Robert A. Wilson. *Ishtar Rising: Or, Why the Goddess Went to Hell and What to Expect Now That She's Returning* (New York: New Falcon Publications, 1988).

"Isis is a popular iteration . . ."—Margot Adler. *Drawing Down the Moon: Witches, Druids, Goddess-Worshippers, and Other Pagans in America Today*, revised and expanded edition (New York: Beacon Press, 1986).

"She was associated with the . . ."—Margot Adler. *Drawing Down the Moon: Witches, Druids, Goddess-Worshippers, and Other Pagans in America Today*, revised and expanded edition (New York: Beacon Press, 1986).

"In the myth, Isis travels" . . .—Jaime Alvar. *Romanising Oriental Gods: Myth, Salvation, and Ethics in the Cults of Cybele, Isis, and Mithras* (Boston: Brill, 2008).

"With Inanna, she retrieves Dumuzi after . . ."—Jaime Alva., *Romanising Oriental Gods: Myth, Salvation, and Ethics in the Cults of Cybele, Isis, and Mithras* (Boston: Brill, 2008).

"Aphrodite was associated with the . . ."—Jeremy Black and Anthony Green. *Gods, Demons and Symbols of Ancient Mesopotamia: An Illustrated Dictionary* (London: British Museum Press, 1992).

"A goddess of beauty, romance . . ."—Jeremy Black and Anthony Green. *Gods, Demons and Symbols of Ancient Mesopotamia: An Illustrated Dictionary* (London: British Museum Press, 1992).

"Many paintings depict her either . . ."—Caroline Arscott and Katie Scott. *Manifestations of Venus: Art and Sexuality* (Manchester, UK: Manchester University Press, 2000).

"Temples of Aphrodite abounded including . . ."—Joseph Campbell. *Occidental Mythology: The Masks of God* (New York: Penguin, 1991).

"It has stood since the . . ."—Joseph Campbell. *Occidental Mythology: The Masks of God* (New York: Penguin, 1991).

"Freja was a Norse goddess . . ."—Hilda Ellis Davidson. *Roles of the Northern Goddess*, (Abingdon, UK: Routledge, 1998).

"She was a governess of . . ."—Hilda Ellis Davidson. *Roles of the Northern Goddess* (Abingdon, UK: Routledge, 1998).

"Married to the god Odin . . ."—Hilda Ellis Davidson. *Roles of the Northern Goddess* (Abingdon, UK: Routledge, 1998).

"The goddess was thought to . . ."—M. Beard, S. Price, and J. North. *Religions of Rome. Volume 1: A History, Illustrated* (Cambridge, UK: Cambridge University Press, 1998).

"She also was known to . . ."—M. Beard, S. Price, and J. North. *Religions of Rome. Volume 1: A History, Illustrated* (Cambridge, UK: Cambridge University Press, 1998).

"In the Aeneid, the hero . . ."—Virgil, *The Aeneid* (New York: Vintage Books, 1993).

"The author, Virgil, also cites . . ."—Virgil, *The Aeneid* (New York: Vintage Books, 1993).

"Some accounts of the goddess . . ."—Clysta Kinstler. *The Moon under Her Feet* (San Francisco: HarperSanFrancisco, 1983).

"She was thought by some . . ."—George Henry Tavard. *The Thousand Faces of the Virgin Mary* (Collegeville, MN: Liturgical Press, 1996).

"She was thought to have . . ."—George Henry Tavard. *The Thousand Faces of the Virgin Mary* (Collegeville, MN: Liturgical Press, 1996).

"Some believe her apprentice Mari . . ."—George Henry Tavard. *The Thousand Faces of the Virgin Mary* (Collegeville, MN: Liturgical Press, 1996).

"Although associated with the Evening . . ."—George Henry Tavard. *The Thousand Faces of the Virgin Mary* (Collegeville, MN: Liturgical Press, 1996).

SHE of Clay and Stars

"The great goddess can change . . ."—Anton Ehrenzweig. *The Hidden Order of Art* (London: University of California Press, Ltd.,1971).

Geography of the Goddess

"According to the Finns, Luonnotar . . ."—Philip Wilkinson. *Illustrated Dictionary of Mythology* (New York: DK Publishing, 2006), 86.

"The Slavs were so steeped in . . ."—Philip Wilkinson. *Illustrated Dictionary of Mythology* (New York: DK Publishing, 2006), 88–89.

"The Celts venerated Nantosuelta, goddess . . ."—Philip Wilkinson. *Illustrated Dictionary of Mythology* (New York: DK Publishing, 2006), 90–91.

"They also embodied the concept . . ."—Philip Wilkinson. *Illustrated Dictionary of Mythology* (New York: DK Publishing, 2006), 90.

"In Fon creation stories, Yewa is . . ."—Philip Wilkinson. *Illustrated Dictionary of Mythology* (New York: DK Publishing, 2006), 114.

"A goddess in Fon creation . . ."—Philip Wilkinson. *Illustrated Dictionary of Mythology* (New York: DK Publishing, 2006), 114.

"The Yoruba people are called . . ."—Philip Wilkinson. *Illustrated Dictionary of Mythology* (New York: DK Publishing, 2006), 115.

"In ancient China, Nu Wa was . . ."—Philip Wilkinson. *Illustrated Dictionary of Mythology* (New York: DK Publishing, 2006), 46.

"Hsi Wang-Mu, also known . . ."—Philip Wilkinson. *Illustrated Dictionary of Mythology* (New York: DK Publishing, 2006), 47.

"In an interesting Indian–Chinese . . ."—Philip Wilkinson. *Illustrated Dictionary of Mythology* (New York: DK Publishing, 2006), 47.

"Uzume was the Shinto goddess . . ."—Philip Wilkinson. *Illustrated Dictionary of Mythology* (New York: DK Publishing, 2006), 50.

"Amaterasu is the goddess of . . ."—Philip Wilkinson. *Illustrated Dictionary of Mythology* (New York: DK Publishing, 2006), 50.

"Benten was the goddess of . . ."—Philip Wilkinson. *Illustrated Dictionary of Mythology* (New York: DK Publishing, 2006), 51.

"Native North Americans are a . . ."—Philip Wilkinson. *Illustrated Dictionary of Mythology* (New York: DK Publishing, 2006), 95.

"The Caribou Inuit people in . . ."—Philip Wilkinson. *Illustrated Dictionary of Mythology* (New York: DK Publishing, 2006), 95.

"One of their most significant . . ."—Philip Wilkinson. *Illustrated Dictionary of Mythology* (New York: DK Publishing, 2006), 96.

"Native peoples who inhabited the . . ."—Philip Wilkinson. *Illustrated Dictionary of Mythology* (New York: DK Publishing, 2006), 100.

"In this same region, the . . ."—Philip Wilkinson. *Illustrated Dictionary of Mythology* (New York: DK Publishing, 2006), 100.

"All throughout North and Central . . ."—Philip Wilkinson. *Illustrated Dictionary of Mythology* (New York: DK Publishing, 2006), 96.

"The Navajo in the Southwest . . ."—Philip Wilkinson. *Illustrated Dictionary of Mythology* (New York: DK Publishing, 2006), 104.

"The Aztec in Central America . . ."—Philip Wilkinson. *Illustrated Dictionary of Mythology* (New York: DK Publishing, 2006), 109.

"The worship of gods and . . ."—Philip Wilkinson. *Illustrated Dictionary of Mythology* (New York: DK Publishing, 2006), 95.

"Mama Kilya was beloved . . ."—Philip Wilkinson. *Illustrated Dictionary of Mythology* (New York: DK Publishing, 2006), 110.

"She also was called a . . ."—Philip Wilkinson. *Illustrated Dictionary of Mythology* (New York: DK Publishing, 2006), 110.

"It was believed that when . . ."—Philip Wilkinson. *Illustrated Dictionary of Mythology* (New York: DK Publishing, 2006), 110.

"Chaska-Qoylor was a star deity . . ."—Philip Wilkinson. *Illustrated Dictionary of Mythology* (New York: DK Publishing, 2006), 111.

"The climate in South America . . ."—Philip Wilkinson. *Illustrated Dictionary of Mythology* (New York: DK Publishing, 2006), 95.

"Pacha Mama was an earth . . ."—Philip Wilkinson. *Illustrated Dictionary of Mythology* (New York: DK Publishing, 2006), 110.

"She was called the giver . . ."—Philip Wilkinson. *Illustrated Dictionary of Mythology* (New York: DK Publishing, 2006), 110.

"In Australia, origin stories and tales . . ."—Philip Wilkinson. *Illustrated Dictionary of Mythology* (New York: DK Publishing, 2006), 119.

"The Yolngu people passed along . . ."—Philip Wilkinson. *Illustrated Dictionary of Mythology* (New York: DK Publishing, 2006), 121.

"Hine-Te-Wauin was the Polynesian goddess . . ."—Philip Wilkinson. *Illustrated Dictionary of Mythology* (New York: DK Publishing, 2006), 122.

"The Maori called their Mother . . ."—Philip Wilkinson. *Illustrated Dictionary of Mythology* (New York: DK Publishing, 2006), 122.

"Pele was the fire and volcano . . ."—Philip Wilkinson. *Illustrated Dictionary of Mythology* (New York: DK Publishing, 2006), 123.

Inner Temple

"For example, in the Sanctuary . . ."—Anneli Rufus and Kristan Lawson. *Goddess Sites: Europe* (New York: HarperCollins, 1991.)

"At certain points in history . . ."—Emma Mildon. *Evolution of the Goddess* (New York: Enliven Books/Atria, 2018), 74.

"In those villages, all the women . . ."—Emma Mildo. *Evolution of the Goddess* (New York: Enliven Books/Atria, 2018), 73–74.

"They would be attended to . . ."—Emma Mildon. *Evolution of the Goddess* (New York: Enliven Books/Atria, 2018), 74.

"Physiologically, that is because at . . ."—Kathy Maupin. *The Secret Female Hormone* (New York: Hay House. 2015).

Goddess Meditations and Activities

"Water helps everything in the . . ."—F. Batmanghelidj. *Your Body's Many Cries for Water* (Falls Church: Global Health Solutions, Inc., 2008).

ACKNOWLEDGMENTS

So many extraordinary goddess women have shaped my life, from my mother, grandmothers, aunts, and cousins to my magnificent friends. Their examples, their support, and their camaraderie mean the world to me. All that divine feminine energy in my life is a big part of why I do what I do.

I am grateful to my medicine teacher Levity Laughing Star, who provided a sound foundation upon which I could build my own medicine work. The words for the seal and protect part of the Goddess Meditation for Protection were based on something shared with me by Levity. I am also thankful to Levity's teacher Twyla for the experiences I talk about in Chapter 5.

My good fortune continues in the form of my executive assistant, Karen Nino. This lovely goddess functions as everything from a marketing assistant to a research assistant and everything in between. It is with the support of this lovely goddess and so many other wonderful women that this book was created.

In seventh grade, my life was graced by a nurturing teacher named Mrs. Broussard. She ignited my imagination with stories of mythology and ancient civilizations and started a lifelong love affair with mythological goddesses for me. What a gift! She also had all of us in her class write a letter to our eighteen-year-old selves, seal it, and write our home address on it. Six years later, when we were seniors, those letters showed up in the mail. Mrs. Broussard is the definition of what it means to be an exemplary and dedicated teacher.

She got a learning-disabled, distractible dreamer engaged in class with her teaching talent.

The adage that it takes a village to rear a child also applies to the process of creating a book baby. I have been incredibly fortunate to partner with such an exemplary village as the team at Sterling. With a commitment to excellence, they have made our works of art. I am so grateful to the design team at Sterling who makes every book gorgeous, including Gina Bonanno. All the committee members who say yes to my projects, please accept my gratitude.

A big part of that Sterling good fortune is getting to work with Kate Zimmerman. She is an editor extraordinaire, and more than that, it means the world to me that she's been able to see my vision and has worked with me to create something so much better than what I originally conceived every time. Ashten "Luna" Evans has been a joyous addition to the editorial team. She continues the tradition of greatness and quality that Sterling brings. Working with her is an absolute dream.

I am fortunate to have a bunch of powerhouse goddesses, including Krystin White, Carolyn Joyce, and Sarah Hall at Sarah Hall Productions, getting the word out about my books.

The woman who makes this all possible and makes my dreams come true again and again is my sweet, kind, and gently badass literary agent, Lisa Hagan. She is certainly an embodiment of the goddess walking among us. I'm not sure how I got so lucky. Lisa is kind of like Lakshmi, opening doors and paving the way for golden opportunities. Thank you, Lisa.

INDEX

113

ABOUT THE AUTHOR

Amy Leigh Mercree is a best-selling author of eleven books, a speaker, an internationally renowned medical intuitive, and a holistic health expert. Mercree teaches internationally, sharing Meet Your Guides, Bestseller Bootcamp, online Mindfulness and Mediation, New Moon Goddess Bootcamp, and Goddess Shamanism classes.

Mercree is the author of *The Spiritual Girl's Guide to Dating*, *A Little Bit of Chakras*, *Joyful Living: 101 Ways to Transform Your Spirit and Revitalize Your Life*, *The Chakras and Crystals Cookbook*, *The Compassion Revolution: 30 Days of Living from the Heart*, *A Little Bit of Meditation*, *Essential Oils Handbook*, *Apple Cider Vinegar Handbook*, *A Little Bit of Mindfulness*, and *The Mood Book: Crystals, Oils, and Rituals to Elevate Your Spirit*.

Mercree has been featured in *Glamour Magazine*, *Women's Health*, *Inc. Magazine*, *Shape*, *The Huffington Post*, *Your Tango*, *Soul and Spirit Magazine*, *Mind Body Green*, CBS, NBC, Hello Giggles, *Reader's Digest*, *Bustle*, *Country Living*, *Forbes*, Oprah.com, and many more.

To get your free Goddess Toolkit and start living as the goddess you truly are, go to AmyLeighMercree.com/goddesstoolkit and enter the password GODDESS.